The Service Member's Guide to Deployment

What every Soldier, Sailor, Airman and Marine should know prior to being deployed

Thomas A. Mengesha
Captain, United States Army Reserve

The Mengesha Publishing Co.

The Mengesha Publishing Co.
26677 West Twelve Mile Road
Southfield, MI 48034
www.mengesha.com

Copyright ©2009, Thomas A. Mengesha
All rights reserved.

ISBN-10 0-9818378-0-8
ISBN-13 978-0-9818378-0-2
Copyright information available upon request.

Cover Design: Robert L. Gatewood
Interior Design: J. L. Saloff
Editing: Trina R. Mengesha, Esq.
Typography: Adobe Garamond Pro

Except in the United States of America, this book is sold subject to the condition that it shall not, by way of trade or otherwise, be lent, resold, hired out, or otherwise circulated without the publisher's prior consent in any form of binding or cover other than that in which it is published and without a similar condition including this condition being imposed on the subsequent purchaser.

The scanning, uploading and distribution of this book via the Internet or via any other means without permission of the publisher is illegal and punishable by law. Please purchase only authorized electronic editions, and do not participate in or encourage electronic piracy of copyrighted materials. Your support of the author's rights is appreciated.

v. 1.0
First Edition, 2009
Printed on acid free paper.

CONTENTS

Why A Book on Deployment? 1

Introduction. 3

PART 1: Get Ready For The Ride! 5
Family Care Plan. 11
Selecting a Financial Institution 13
Medical Insurance Enrollment 14
TRICARE Coverage 14
SGLI Life Insurance 15
The Power of a Power of Attorney 17
Family Support Programs During Deployment 20

Operation Military Child Care 20
Military One Source 21
Health Care, Hospice, and Recovery Organizations. 26
Advice to the Families of Deployed Service Members 27
Create a Virtual You! 30
Employer Support of the Guard and Reserve. 31
Self-Employed Service Members 32
Service Members Civil Relief Act 33
Move out! 36

PART 2: Mobilization Station 39

Global War on Terror 44
Mobilization Station Processing 44
LNO/Installation Team Support 45
Warrior Task Training. 46
Additional MOS/AOC Training 46
Unit Assignment Instructions. 46
Expected Processing/Training Period. 47
(The Mobilization Station's) Commitment to You 47
Keep Document Copies/Provide to HRC-STL 48
Communication is Key 48
Making the Most of Your Time During Mobilization 49

Contents / v

PART 3: A Time of New Beginnings! 53
    RIP/TOA. 60
    Kuwait Deployments v Iraq Deployments 62
Taking Advantage of Special Benefits While Deployed . . . 63
    Financial Benefits. 63
    A Breakdown of your Pay While Deployed 64
    Family Separation Allowance (FSA). 64
    Hostile Fire/Imminent Danger Pay (HF/IDP) 65
    Combat Zone Tax Exclusion (CZTE). 65
    Basic Allowance for Subsistence (BAS) 66
    Basic Allowance for Housing (BAH) 66
    Reenlistment Bonus 67
    Special Leave Accrual (SLA) 67
    MY PAY 67
Savings and Investment Programs 68
    TSP. 68
    Savings Deposit Program. 68
Rest and Recuperation. 73
    R & R Passes. 76
    The USO 78
Becoming a U.S. Citizen. 88
    Peacetime Military Service 88
    Service During Hostilities 89

Posthumous Citizenship 89
Making the Most of Your Time During Deployment 91
Cards, Letters, Gifts, and Care Packages 95
    America Supports You 97
    Subscriptions for Service Members 97
Lessons Learned 98
    CRISP Yard 98
    Voting while deployed 100
    Service Members and their Political Activities 102
Prisoner of War 107
Battlefield stress 111
Death 112
    What happens to personal affects of the deceased
    service member? 114
Improve your foxhole 114
    Financial Liability Investigation of
    Property Lost (FLIPL) 116

PART 4: "Pop Smoke!" 119
    DCS Briefing 121
    Travel Vouchers 122

PART 5: Mission Accomplished 127
Reuniting with family 134
Post-Deployment Resources and Support 135
Outward Bound Wilderness Excursions for Operations Enduring and Iraqi Freedom Veterans 135
Transition, Scholarships and Vocation Rehabilitation .. 136
Counseling and Other Relief and Support Organizations 137
Post Deployment/Mobilization Respite Absence Program 139

Conclusion: A Snowflake in the Desert 141
Final Thoughts 147

Sources 149

Tom and Admiral Mike Mullen, Chairman of the Joint Chiefs of Staff.

Dedication

This book is dedicated to the millions of service members that have been deployed in defense of America's freedoms, and the millions more who have yet to be deployed to fight for liberty and freedom not only in America but around the world. Your sacrifice is truly appreciated by millions of people around the world who desire to be free.

To my father, SFC -Retired- Nathaniel Rainey, Sr. who inspired me to join the United States Army as a young boy growing up on Pawley's Island, South Carolina. He was the best chef the military ever had! No one has ever topped his pinto beans and rice. My favorite dish!

To LTC Gregory A. Kent who taught me everything about grace, courage, friendship and honor. You sir are the standard for what is right with military leadership! Thank you for the support, guidance and mentoring you provided me. You will never be forgotten.

To SGM Charles (RED BADGE!) James—My true friend and mentor in Kuwait. Thanks for everything!

To Philip J. Thomas, Esq.—The lawyers' Lawyer! You sir are a good man! philipJthomas@aol.com.

To my loving wife Trina—My partner in life. May God continue to bless our family. I love you!

To all my children—Angelica, Thomas II, Marissa and Troy. The best children any parent could ask for! I love you all very much!

Tom preparing for a training mission, Fort McCoy in Wisconsin.

WHY A BOOK ON DEPLOYMENT?

During Captain Mengesha's two-year deployment, and serving in critical positions, it was discovered that soldiers were lacking valuable information which would enable them and their families to transition more smoothly into their deployments.

Realizing that very few, if any, books were available to address this need, Captain Mengesha decided to put together an informative, easy-to-read guide book to provide as much information as possible to service members so that they would be prepared for all aspects of the deployment process. This information is critical to ensure a smooth transition for the soldier, and to prepare their families for what to expect and how to take advantage of crucial benefits and resources available.

"If this book helps just one service member be better prepared for the stresses of a deployment to a combat and war zone, then I will have done my job!"
—Captain Thomas A. Mengesha, Attorney at Law

Tom at his desk in Camp Beuhring.

Introduction

So you have learned that you are about to be deployed! There may be many different emotions you now feel. You may be scared. You may be excited. Or maybe you do not know how to feel. One thing is certain; your life will never be quite the same. Soon reality will set in and you will wonder to yourself, what am I suppose to do now? How will my family be taken care of? What will happen to my job? If you are self-employed, you may wonder what will happen to my business? What should I expect while deployed?

If you are a family member of the deploying service member, you may be wondering how you will be able to contact your loved one while they are deployed? What will happen if there is a family emergency? Most of all you may wonder if and how you will be able to stay in contact either as a deployed service member or the family of the deployed service member?

This book was written for the service member and their family! After reading this book, these as well as other questions will be answered, giving you a greater sense of comfort during this stressful time of uncertainty.

PART 1
GET READY FOR THE RIDE!

Tom flying over the Iraq border.

There are certain events in a person's life that when they occur, leave an indelible imprint on their life. For some it was the assassination of Dr. Martin Luther King, Jr. for others it was the assassination of President John F. Kennedy. The event for me was the September 11, 2001 terrorist attacks on the United States.

I remember that day like it was yesterday. On September 11, 2001, I was a young attorney practicing law in Flint, Michigan. In fact I had only been practicing law for a little more than two years at the time of the attacks. My practice focused on Criminal Law, Family Law as well as a few other areas. On that fateful day I was representing a client in family court on a child neglect matter. As I recall, I was sitting in Judge Farah's court room (one of the family court judges) when all of a sudden one of my colleagues ran into the court room and stated that a plane flew into one of the twin towers in New

York City. Little did my collegue and I realize the full gravity of the situation. I left Judge Farah's courtroom and went back to my office. Downstairs from my office was the headquarters of the Genesee County Bar Association. From there I watched both towers fall as did millions of other Americans on the television that morning.

I remember remarking to Angie Lewis (my administrative assistant at the time and the "brains" behind my law firm) that I might be deployed soon because of the attacks and to start making plans in case I was in fact deployed. My deployment did come, but not for some 5 years later.

The sequence of events on September 11, 2001 changed America forever. On that day, The United States of America lost its innocence. The land of the free was no longer as free as it once was. Open and free travel no longer seemed as open and free following the September 11th terrorist attacks. Subsequently, America soon found itself at war with Iraq and Afghanistan. The number of service members needed to adequately fight the war was tremendous. The numbers of service members on active duty were not enough to engage in effective combat. As such, the burden to pick up the slack fell upon the Reserve and National Guard forces of our military. Not in recent memory has there been a greater number of service members deployed stateside or over seas (CONUS or OCONUS). From a military development standpoint, the wars in Iraq and Afghanistan provoked the number of deployments to grow substantially. Since September 11, 2001, over 1.7 million service members have been deployed in support of Operation Iraqi Freedom (OIF) and Operation Enduring

Freedom (OEF). Operation Enduring Freedom's military focus is on securing the nation of Afghanistan, while as its name suggest, Operation Iraqi Freedom is concerned with securing the nation of Iraq. In addition to the service members deployed to Iraq and Afghanistan, thousands of service members were deployed to Kuwait and Qatar in support of Operations Iraqi Freedom and Enduring Freedom. Moreover, tens of thousands of service members were deployed in support of contingency operations around the world.

★   ★   ★

So what happens when you receive your "orders" to go? Generally speaking, your Unit, if you are deploying as a unit, will receive unit orders informing the Command that their unit will be deployed. If on the other hand you are deployed as an individual, as I was, you could receive your initial order via a phone call followed by orders requesting that you report for active duty. The amount of notice given to a service member ranges anywhere from several months in advance to only several days prior to the date ordered to active duty. I received my orders only three weeks before my scheduled date to report for duty.

There have been millions of Americans deployed to war zones around the world since this great country was founded over 230 years ago, however, it appears that many soldiers are deploying in greater frequency than ever before. In addition, some of those deployed are on their 2nd, 3rd, 4th and even 5th deployment. In many cases the deployment is involuntary and not having critical information to make the deployment less stressful creates a tremendous burden not only for the deploying service member but the family of that service member as well.

Deployment is much like a roller coaster ride at an amusement park. You first have the uncertainty of the entire event much like what you feel as you enter the gate to a roller coaster that you have never ridden before. You are unsure if you will make it. You may even attempt to get out of it at the very last minute. The roller coaster makes its climb and just as you begin the process of family planning and the actual deployment in the military, you become anxious and nervous. After you've made it to the top of the roller coaster, you brace yourself for your quick descent, and at this point you realize there is no turning back. This is a similar feeling to what you may experience upon reaching your mobilization site but you brace yourself anyway

Combat training at Fort McCoy, in Wisconsin.

and prepare for the many highs and lows this ride will offer.

It is my intent that after reading this book, service members and their families will come away with a greater understanding of what is in store for them during the deployment and the best ways to minimize the difficulties that they will encounter.

FAMILY CARE PLAN

One of the first things a service member should do prior to deployment is review and/or implement a family care plan. Your family care plan should be reviewed certainly if you are being deployed, but also at least once a year regardless of deployment status. It is said, "The strength of the Family is the strength of the Soldier is the strength of the Military is the strength of the Nation!" So it logically follows that caring and providing for the families of service members alleviates many of the stresses related to deployment and combat. This in turn leads to the strong national defense of the United States of America.

The very first thing you should do upon learning that you are going to be deployed is to inform the family and start making a plan. Regardless if you have children or not, you should have some form of a Family Care Plan in place.

One of the most important considerations of family readiness is to ensure that your family is taken care of during times of drills, annual training, mobilization and deployment. A Family Care Plan is very important for all families, and is especially critical for single parents and dual military parents.

A Family Care Plan should be developed whether you

expect to be deployed or not; in fact many units will require you to develop a formal Family Care Plan. Taking care of these considerations now will help you and your family be prepared for any period of separation.

When you prepare your plan, be sure to do the following:

- ★ Assign a guardian for your family in a special Power of Attorney and make sure that the guardian understands his/her responsibilities.
- ★ Obtain ID and commissary cards, register in DEERS, and check to make sure all ID cards have not expired.
- ★ Sign up for SGLI or a similar group life insurance, and update all beneficiary information.
- ★ Arrange for housing, food, transportation and emergency needs.
- ★ Inform your spouse or any caretakers about your financial matters.
- ★ Arrange for your guardian to have access to necessary funds.
- ★ Arrange for child care, education and medical care.
- ★ Prepare a will, and designate a guardian in the will.
- ★ Arrange for necessary travel and escort to

transfer family members to their guardian.

★ Discuss your plans with your older children.[1]

The overall financial picture of the family should be discussed and understood by the entire family. It is amazing how many couples do not discuss the family bills and their overall finances. One spouse may have been responsible for handling the family finances, and the other may have no idea about what gets paid and to whom. It is imperative that both spouses are aware of all bills, when they are due, as well as the overall financial well being of the family. The down side of not knowing the full financial picture of the family finances is that when the person responsible gets deployed, bills may unknowingly go unpaid resulting in default issuances and thus affecting your credit.

SELECTING A FINANCIAL INSTITUTION

One of the most important decisions a service member can make prior to deployment is the selection of a financial institution. Selecting a good financial institution is very important, as there are many things to consider relating to financial transactions during your deployment. Some things to consider when selecting a financial institution include, ease of use, the ability to make wire transfers, and accessing your bank account online just to name a few things. Remember, as a deployed service member you will be traveling to remote parts of the earth. As such you want to ensure that your financial institution can be accessed via the Internet.

It is important that you shop around for a financial institution that knows how the military functions and if possible provides benefits for service members at a reduced cost. There are quite a few such financial institutions out there. I have tried many. Of all that I have tried, I can say without reservation that USAA Federal Savings Bank (USAA) is the absolute best. They are second to none in my opinion. They have a great on-line banking program that includes USAA Deposit@Home, 24/7 access to your accounts, USAA Web BillPay as well as other great services. Their website is www.usaa.com. However, the choice is yours to make.

MEDICAL INSURANCE ENROLLMENT

Medical and health insurance is very important and is one of the key benefits given to active duty service members and their families. As such, the military has an excellent medical program to take care of family members during a deployment. Tricare is the medical program for the military.

TRICARE COVERAGE

Once a service member is alerted, both the service member and their family members are entitled to submit claims for recent medical expenses (for reimbursement only) to TRICARE (the military's medical care system) for medical expenses incurred up to 90 days prior to the reporting date on the mobilization orders. Full family medical coverage under TRICARE starts the first day of mobilization/active duty.

Family members should obtain ID cards as soon as possible by bringing a copy of the mobilization orders (and identification/copy of marriage license) to the nearest ID card issuance facility. ID cards are available through any military installation and most Reserve Centers and National Guard Armories with ID card and Defense Enrollment Eligibility Reporting System (DEERS) access. A listing of these installations is at the TRICARE DEERS information web site:

http://www.tricare.osd.mil/deers/default.cfm

It is important that family members be entered into the DEERS database as quickly as possible (which occurs upon ID card issuance), as this is how the military verifies family member eligibility for support, services and entitlements, including TRICARE.[2]

ID cards contain all of the information necessary related to the service member (or sponsor) for medical coverage for spouses and dependents. Therefore, enrolling in DEERS as soon as possible cannot be stressed enough.

SGLI Life Insurance

Life Insurance is a very important and valuable benefit for service members. At the time of writing this book, service members who died while on active duty received up to $400,000 and under certain situations could receive even more money. Servicemembers' Group Life Insurance or SGLI is a government life insurance policy the covers service members who die or are killed. The money is paid directly to the named beneficiary or beneficiaries upon the death of the service member. This money could also be used to fund a Trust. In such a case, the trustee would then carry out the wishes of the deceased service member. Additionally, there are other monies paid to the family upon the death of a service member in combat. I will discuss those benefits in greater detail later in the book.

It is very important that as a service member you review your SGLI policy to update beneficiary information or make necessary modifications. A thorough review of your insurance policy is a must and should be done yearly regardless of your deployment status. You need to review your beneficiary information just in case something unfortunate happens to you the service member. You want to make certain that the person receiving the death benefit actually is the intended recipient or beneficiary. You certainly want to ensure your intended beneficiary is provided for if you are killed while serving our country.

I know of several cases where, because the service member did not update their SGLI policy, an ex-spouse or someone other than the intended beneficiary received the insurance money. In situations like that, there is little the intended beneficiary can do, especially without court intervention. Even then, the intended beneficiary has very little to adequately show they were the intended beneficiary. Think of it this way, if it were that easy to contest the named beneficiary, courts would be tied up more than they are already with cases of folks trying to overturn what the court assumes is the "will" of the deceased. If you believe that you were the intended beneficiary of a deceased service member's life insurance benefits, contact an attorney immediately to discuss all of your possible options.

The Power of a Power of Attorney

As noted above, one of the first things you want to do upon notice of your impending deployment is to notify family and loved ones. However, of great importance is the preparation and safekeeping of a power of attorney. Never underestimate the power of a power of attorney!

When considering securing a power of attorney, know that there are two types. A special power of attorney and a general power of attorney. A general power of attorney gives another person broad and far reaching authority to handle your affairs. A special power of attorney only provides for specifically limited handling of your affairs such as selling your vehicle or preparing your taxes. Regardless of the type of power of attorney you give, there should be a specific termination date. As an attorney, I recommend that powers of attorney terminate after one year has passed.

The following two "case scenarios" should provide a better illustration of the power of power of attorneys.

Case Scenario 1:
"Service Member" was ordered to active duty to be deployed to Iraq in support of Operation Iraqi Freedom. "Service Member" has been married for 18 years to a wonderful person, "Spouse".

"Service Member" loved "Spouse" very much and wanted to ensure "Spouse" was able to take care of things in "Service Member's" absence. Prior to "Service Member" departing for duty "Spouse" was given a Power of Attorney.

Do to the stress and temptations of "Service Member's" absence, "Spouse" files for divorce. However, due to "Service Member" not fully understanding the difference between a general power of attorney and a special power of attorney, "Service Member" gave "Spouse" a general power of attorney.

What do you think happened? In this case scenario, "Spouse" was given a general power of attorney. As such "Spouse" had far reaching authority to act on behalf of "Service Member". "Spouse" was able to withdraw $10,000.00 from "Service Member's" bank account, sell "Service Members" 1965 Cobra, and withdraw money at will from "Service Member's" bank account. "Spouse" did this while filing for divorce from "Service Member" and receiving all of the military housing allowance that totaled nearly $2,000.00 per month. Needless to say that upon "Service Member's" return from deployment, "Service Member" was depressed and had to seek counseling. Not to mention all of "Service Member's" assets were gone and "Service Member" had little recourse as "Service Member" gave "Spouse" a general power of attorney.

Case Scenario 2:

"Service Member" was ordered to active duty to be deployed to Afghanistan in support of Operation Enduring Freedom. "Service Member" has been married for 5 years to a wonderful person, "Spouse".

"Service Member" loved "Spouse" very much and wanted to ensure "Spouse" was able to take care of things in "Service Member's" absence. Prior to "Service Member" departing for duty "Spouse" was given a Power of Attorney.

Do to the stress and temptations of "Service Member's" absence, "Spouse" files for divorce. However, prior to deploying to Afghanistan, "Service Member" read the book *The Service Member's Guide to Deployment; what every Soldier, Sailor, Airmen and Marine should know prior to being deployed.* Copyright 2008 by CPT Thomas A. Mengesha "Service Member" gave "Spouse" a special power of attorney.

What do you think happened? In this case scenario, "Service Member", though unhappy about getting a divorce, was very happy about obtaining a special power of attorney to handle the very limited duty of ensuring taxes were paid during the absence of the deployment. With a special power of attorney, the person who receives the power can only carry out the specific instructions laid out in the document.

Remember, it is easier to add or broaden the power than cut back, particularly if the person who has the general power of attorney is acting in bad faith. These are just hypothetical scenarios to illustrate how powers of attorney may be used. In most cases, trusted spouses and family members may be given a power of attorney to enable them to make important decisions on your behalf during your absence. However, if you have any doubts about the trustworthiness of an individual, be cautious about giving a power of attorney.

FAMILY SUPPORT PROGRAMS DURING DEPLOYMENT

There are some great organizations and programs available to assist the families during deployment. Unfortunately many service members do not know about them. That was a problem I had when I deployed. Despite all the training I had on personnel matters, there was still a great deal of information I was unaware of.

Operation Military Child Care

If you have children, this is an outstanding program that provides assistance with childcare expenses in the form of subsidy payments for families of deployed service members. The program basics are as follows:

- ★ Provide child care fee assistance for National Guard and Reserve service members who are activated or deployed and whose children are enrolled in non-DoD licensed child care programs
- ★ Provide child care fee assistance for deployed, Active-Duty Military (Army, Marine Corps, Navy, and Air Force) whose children are enrolled in non-DoD-licensed child care programs

Eligibility

★ Families/legal guardians of the children of National Guard & Reserve Service Members who are currently activated/deployed are eligible

★ Families/legal guardians of the children of deployed Active Duty Soldiers, Marines, Sailors, and Airmen who are unable to access child care on military installations are eligible

Program Benefits

★ Help locating licensed child care options in your community

★ Reduced child care fees, through a subsidy

★ Eligible to participate during the period of the Service Member's deployment period and for 60 days after the return of the Service Member

★ Provide a subsidy for 60 days while a non-military spouse is looking for work[3]

Military One Source

One of the greatest resources to assist the families of deployed service members can be found on the World Wide Web. Military One Source's stated mission taken directly from their website states the following:

> *"Whether it is help with child care, personal finances, emotional support during deployments, relocation information, or resources needed for special circumstances, Military One Source is there for military personnel and their families... 24/7/365!"*

The service is available by phone, online and face-to-face through private counseling sessions in the local community. Highly qualified, master's prepared consultants provide the service. Personalized consultations on specific issues such as education, special needs, and finances are provided. Customized research detailing community resources and appropriate military referrals are offered. Clients can even get help with simultaneous language interpretation and document translation services.

The interactive Web site includes locator's for education, child care, and elder care, online articles, referrals to military and community resources, financial calculators, live online workshops called Webinars, and "E-mail a consultant." Additional resources include brief videos of consultants addressing common issues such as communicating as a couple, budgeting and managing anger.

Face-to-face counseling sessions focus on issues such as normal reactions to abnormal situations (e.g. combat), couples concerns, work/life balance, grief and loss, adjustment to deployment, stress management, and parenting. Persons seeking counseling will receive up to six counseling sessions per issue at no cost to them. To access a counselor in the local community, individuals may call a Military OneSource consultant directly.

Service is available in CONUS as well as Hawaii, Alaska, U.S. Virgin Islands and Puerto Rico.

Military OneSource is provided by the Department of Defense at no cost to active duty, Guard and Reserve (regardless of activation status) and their families.[4]

Military One Source has and continues to serve as a treasure trove of information to assist service members during their deployments to the Iraq War Theater of Operations. It is important to note that Military One Source is not just for deployed service members but for all military personnel. I strongly encourage everyone to visit the site and familiarize themselves with the resources available through this organization. You are sure to find something for everyone.

Tom and gunner, returning with flag flown over Iraq.

Our Military Kids[5]

Another great program that will actually pay for your child's development while you are deployed is called Our Military Kids (OMK). This program provides tangible support to the children of deployed and severely injured National Guard and Military Reserve personnel through grants for enrichment activities and tutoring that nurture and sustain the children during the time a parent is away in service to our country. "OMK grants are made to honor the sacrifices military parents make and to ensure that the children have access to activities and support that help the children better cope with challenges arising during a parent's deployment or injury recovery."

The following are some highlights and specifics pertaining to the program:

- ★ Grants are available for children aged 3 through 12 up to $500 per award
- ★ Family income is not considered in awarding grants
- ★ Grants may not be used for day care charges
- ★ Each child in a family is eligible to apply for an award up to $500.
- ★ Two grants per year may be awarded per child.

Below is a listing of the types of activities taken from their website that can be funded:[6]

YOUTH SPORTS		
Baseball	Gymnastics	Rowing
Basketball	Horseback Riding	Skiing/Snowboarding
Bowling	Ice Hockey	Soccer
Boxing	Ice Skating	Softball
Cheerleading	In-Line Hockey	Street Hockey
Cross Country	Judo	Swimming
Cycling	Lacrosse	Tennis
Dancing	Martial Arts	Track & Field
Field Hockey	Motorcross	Volleyball
Football	Raquetball/Handball/	Wrestling
Floor Hockey	Squash	Yoga
Golf		

FINE ARTS	TUTORING*	OTHER
Choir/Voice	Reading	Boys & Girls Club
Dance	Math	Chess
Music	English	Creative Thinking
Performing Arts	Writing	Driver Education
Sculpture	Study Skills	Modeling /
Theater	Leadership Training	Beauty Pagents
		School Trips
		Scouting
		Space Camp

*Tutor programs (assisting children to maintain performance at grade level.)

Visit www.ourmilitarykids.org for full details about this outstanding program and its benefits.

Health Care, Hospice, and Recovery Organizations

Should you or your family need medical care or support services, here are some organizations that can help:

- ★ **American Red Cross Armed Forces**—Offers medical services to active duty, veterans, reservists and families nationwide.

- ★ **Blinded Veterans Association**—Volunteer and scholarship organization provides care and support for blind veterans and their families.

- ★ **CAUSE: Comfort for America's Uniformed Services Elite**—Provides comfort items for troops recuperating in military hospitals and rehabilitation centers from wounds and injuries.

- ★ **Fisher House**—Support families whose loved ones are being treated at military and VA hospitals.

- ★ **Military Pets Foster Project**—Nationwide network of foster homes cares for the pets of deployed personnel.

- ★ **Sacred Heart Lodge**—Provides a cost free hassle free vacation to those Soldier's who are returning from War to reconnect to their Families.

★ **The Walter Reed Society**—Walter Reed Society helps provide for the needs of many returning injured service members and their families

ADVICE TO THE FAMILIES OF DEPLOYED SERVICE MEMBERS

Deployments have a very stressful impact on marriages and relationships. One thing that can never be understated is the importance of a strong family support system available to the deployed soldier. I am reminded of my supervisor I had while serving in Kuwait in Support of Operation Iraqi freedom.

LTC Gregory Kent, the Chief of Theater Rest and Recuperation for the wars in Iraq and Afghanistan, was the finest officer I have ever known and a great friend and mentor. During the time I served with him as his Deputy I would never forget to see the smile that came to his face as he would receive letters EVERY day from his wife. Often times he would receive care pack-

LTC Greg Kent and Beam (an executive for Al-Shamel travel).

How to Pack a Care Package for Deployed Soldiers

Things You'll Need:
- Boxes
- Goodies
- Customs Form

Step 1

The first step is knowing what to send them. Here are some of the most requested items: Beef jerky (pork products are forbidden, so keep it beef :) Baby wipes or moist towlets Razors/razor blades Shaving cream Soap Candy (chocolate is pretty hard to send, so you might want to think along the lines of hard candies) Games or books

Step 2

Once you have the goodies together, you will need the boxes. You can get "flat rate boxes" in two sized from the post office, and the great thing about these boxes is that it costs less than $9 to ship it regardless of weight. You can go to www.usps.com and order these free boxes. They will be delivered to your door for no charge, so you can always have some on hand.

Step 3

You need to remember that the mail service to US service members overseas in combat zones is not a perfect service. Boxes get lost, squished, and may sit at larger bases for weeks before being delivered to the smaller bases were you soldier is. Don't put in anything valuable, fragile or perishable. If you need to pad items that are fragile—use rolls of toilet paper—for anyone who has ever used military-issue toiled paper, you understand this.

Step 4

You need to fill out a customs form for any packages going overseas. You can get these from www.usps.com, and have it filled out and ready to go when you get to the post office. Tape you box up well, take your filled-out customs form with you, and head off to the post office. Your soldier, sailor or airmen will thank you!

Tips & Warnings

Alcohol and explicit material is prohibited, as well as pork items.[7]

ages. Sometimes he would receive as many as 3 and 4 letters a day. Now I am not saying everyone has to be as attentive to their spouse, friend or partner but understand this, it made a world of difference to him and his morale. Moreover, that joy was infectious to all who were around LTC Greg Kent!

Now this relationship was not a one-way street. LTC Kent would call his wife daily. He looked forward to making his call and I am certain his wife appreciated them.

I know that this may not be something that is available to all deployed soldiers but one thing is certain I am sure it helped his marriage and may have even made it stronger. People in love have always told me that it is the little things that show the other person that you care. A simple letter is just that. I would also state to everyone that while e-mails are better than nothing, there is nothing like receiving a letter or better yet a "Care Package" during "mail call" hours. That is truly a morale boaster!

You may be asking what are Care Packages? Well I am glad you asked! Care packages are a favorite among deployed soldiers. During my deployment I came across some excellent resources that gave some easy instructions on how to put one of these treasure troves of goodies together. It was written for service members deployed to Iraq and Afghanistan, however, it does provide some good tips for service members deployed around the world.

LTC Kent in his gas mask.

Create a Virtual You!

A tip that I would like to give, particularly if you have small children, is to create a DVD of you speaking or maybe even reading your child's favorite book. Doing so will give that child repeated opportunities to see you. Remember children have emotions and this is certainly a difficult time for them. I know that both my daughter Marissa and son Troy appreciated seeing me and hearing my voice. Even hearing their favorite story told to them on a DVD brought them great joy. Believe me the time you take to do this simple act will pay great dividends in the future.

You should also consider making a special corner of a room dedicated to you. In that area you may want to display a large photo of the deployed service member along with some of their special items that are associated with them like their favorite hat or items of clothing. Doing this provides a "private place" for family members to go on their own to reflect on the service member while away.

Tom resting after negotiating the land navigation course, Fort McCoy.

EMPLOYER SUPPORT OF THE GUARD AND RESERVE

Employer Support of the Guard and Reserve or ESGR is a Department of Defense agency with its stated goal to promote a culture in which all American employers support and value the military service of their employees. This organization recognizes outstanding employer support as well as seeks to increase awareness of the law, and resolve conflicts through mediation. ESGR has three main goals. They are to Inform, Recognize and Mediate.

Informing is accomplished by establishing face to face briefings with the service member, their employer and their unit. The term "Bosslifts" came about from this processes. This gives your employer a first hand experience of the service member's experience of military life. Additional information is provided to the employer such as leave of absence templates, sample letters to employers and USERRA wallet cards through the service members local ESGR field committee and www.esgr.mil

ESGR also recognizes employers who are supportive of their service member worker through the ESGR Patriot Awards program. This award is a great way to tell your boss, "I appreciate your support!". The service member may nominate their boss at: www.esgr.mil

Mediation is a free service offered by ESGR. They provide a professionally-trained Ombudsmen to help clear up misunderstandings between the service member and the employer. It is important to note that ESGR volunteers are available in every state and U.S. territory to provide assistance.

The bottom line is that your civilian job is protected. The Uniformed Services Employment and Reemployment Rights Act (USERRA) is a federal law that protects your civilian job while you serve in the military whether or not you volunteered for duty!

Some key provisions include the following. If you have been deployed for 1-30 days of service, you must return to work the next scheduled day (after safe travel home and 8 hours rest). If you are deployed for 31-180 days, you must reapply for reemployment within 14 days after service completion. If you have been deployed for 181 days or more, then you have to apply for reemployment within 90 days after service completion.

You should know that USERRA has a 5 year job protection limit. The employer is not required to reschedule work missed due to military service and you are not required to find a replacement worker.

Furthermore, USERRA does not require the use of earned vacation to perform military service and USERRA only requires your employer to provide unpaid leave of absence.

For more information contact 1-800-336-4590 or: www.esgr.mil

SELF-EMPLOYED SERVICE MEMBERS

For those of you who are employed, ESGR is a great resource. However, in other cases such as people who are self-employed at the time of their deployment the situation is not as kind. Particularly if you have done nothing to prepare for the loss of your business due to a deployment.

At the time I was deployed, I was the owner and operator of a solo practice private law firm, The Mengesha Firm, P.C. located in Southfield, Michigan.

When I was deployed I lost a significant income. I was the only attorney in my law firm and there was no one to continue the firm's operations during my deployment. You should be aware that at the time of this book being published the military did not have any programs to assist a person in my situation.

My best advice to anyone who is self-employed, in fact everyone, is to have a "rainy day" fund. To the best extent possible, have a plan in place much like a Family Care Plan that would provide for taking care of your business while you are away.

SERVICE MEMBERS CIVIL RELIEF ACT

There are laws that protect service members that are deploying and actually provide for ways to save money. One such law that has many benefits is called the Service Members Civil Relief Act (SCRA).

On 19 December 2003, President Bush signed into law the SCRA. This law is a complete revision of the Soldiers' and Sailors' Civil Relief Act (SSCRA).

The SSCRA provided a number of significant protections to service members. These include: staying court hearings if military service materially affects service members' ability to defend their interests; reducing interest to 6% on pre-service loans and obligations; requiring court action before a service member's family can be evicted from rental property for nonpayment of rent if the monthly rent is $1,200 or less; termination of a pre-service residential lease; and allowing service members to maintain their state of residence for tax purposes despite military relocations to other states.

The SSCRA was largely unchanged from its enactment in 1940. The SCRA was written to: clarify the language of the SSCRA: to incorporate many years of judicial interpretation of the SSCRA; and to update the SSCRA to reflect new developments in American life since 1940.

The New Law:

(1) Extends the application of a service member's right to stay court hearings to administrative hearings. It now requires a court or administrative hearing to grant at least a 90-day stay if requested by the service member. Additional stays can be granted at the discretion of the judge or hearing official.

(2) Clarifies the rules on the 6% interest rate cap on pre-service loans and obligations by specifying that interest in excess of 6% per year must be forgiven. The absence of such language in the SSCRA had allowed some lenders to argue that interest in excess of 6% is merely deferred. It also specifies that a service member must request this reduction in writing and include a copy of his/her orders.

(3) Modifies the eviction protection section by precluding evictions from premises occupied by service members for which

the monthly rent does not exceed $2,400 for the year 2003 (an increase from the current $1,200). The Act provides a formula to calculate the rent ceiling for subsequent years.

(4) Extends the right to terminate real property leases to active duty soldiers moving pursuant to permanent change of station (PCS) orders or deployment orders of at least 90 days. This eliminates the need to request a military termination clause in leases.

(5) Adds a new provision allowing the termination of automobile leases for use by service members and their dependents. Pre-service automobile leases may be cancelled if the service member receives orders to active duty for a period of 180 days or more. Automobile leases entered into while the service member is on active duty may be terminated if the service member receives PCS orders to a location outside the continental United States or deployment orders for a period of 180 days or more.

(6) Adds a provision that would prevent states from increasing the tax bracket of a nonmilitary spouse who earned income in the state by adding in the service member's military income for the limited purpose of determining the nonmilitary spouse's tax bracket. This practice has had the effect of increasing the military family's tax burden.

(7) Adds legal services as a professional service specifically named under the provision that provides for suspension and subsequent reinstatement of existing professional liability insurance coverage for designated professionals serving on active duty. While the SSCRA specifically names only health care services, legal services have been covered since 3 May 1999 by

Secretary of Defense designations. The SSCRA permitted such a Secretarial designation, but this revision will clarify this area.

Historically, the SSCRA applied to members of the National Guard only if they were serving in a Title 10 status. Effective 6 December 2002, the SSCRA protections were extended to members of the National Guard called to active duty for 30 days or more pursuant to a contingency mission specified by the President or the Secretary of Defense. This continues in the SCRA.[8]

Be sure to familiarize yourself with these laws and the protections and benefits that they afford you prior to beginning your deployment.

MOVE OUT!

Now that you have received your Deployment Orders, prepared the family, and made all the arrangements for your deployment, it is time to report to your unit. When I was mobilized in July of 2006, I was known as an Individual Augmentee (IA). That means that I did not deploy with my reserve unit in Southfield, Michigan. Basically what happened is that Department of the Army saw a need that needed to be filled with a deploying unit and filled it. In this case it was filled with me. The unit I deployed with in support of Operation Iraqi Freedom was a personnel unit, The 3rd Personnel Command Forward or 3rd PERSCOM FWD. They were based out of Jackson, Mississippi with a detachment in Columbia, South Carolina. On July 7th, 2006 I reported to my unit in South Carolina.

Now the circle was complete! I returned to my home state of South Carolina for my first deployment to go to war. My return to South Carolina went full circle. It appears that just about every major event in my life has some ties to South Carolina. (I grew up there, graduated from high school and college there, inducted into the Army and was deployed from the great state of South Carolina.)

I remember reporting to my unit very much over weight and out of shape. In fact, I weighed over 300lbs. More on that later.

So there I was back at Fort Jackson in Columbia, South Carolina meeting the rest of the soldiers that I would be deploying with. The time was spent taking care of administrative matters and being measured for uniform and equipment to ensure that once we arrived at our mobilization station, we were issued the correct fitting attire.

Also during this time there were some preliminary matters relating to in processing but of greatest significance looking back was the Deployment Ceremony. The ceremony was very nice. Local political leaders, media and family of those preparing to deploy, attended the deployment ceremony.

I recall during the ceremony the Commanding General awarded the two youngest service members the unit coin. An honor for any deploying service member. The youngest soldiers, two female Privates, had just turned 18 years old.

After the ceremony, political leaders, the media and family left. We were put on "lock down" and prepared for what lay ahead. The ride had now begun!

PART 2
Mobilization Station...
A time to get your
"head in the game"!

Departing to the Middle East.

Once the service member completes their initial in processing with the unit that they will be deploying with, it will be time for their onward travel to their Mobilization Station. After completing my initial in processing and deployment ceremony at Fort Jackson in South Carolina, I departed South Carolina and was flown to Ft. McCoy, Wisconsin to start my training with my unit. I was assigned to the 3rd Personnel Command (Forward) for deployment to the Iraq war theater.

Being sent to a mobilization station is not generic to the Army alone. All service members in some form or another will be sent to a mobilization station for processing prior to being sent into the war zone. You may be wondering what a mobilization station is. Service members who are deployed are sent to what is referred to as a mobilization station. The Department of Defense (DOD) defines a Mobilization Station as "the designated military installation to which a Reserve Component unit or individual is moved for further processing, organizing, equipping, training, and employment and from which the unit or individual may move to an aerial port of embarkation or seaport of embarkation."[9]

If you are wondering what goes on in greater detail during the mobilization station process consider the following:

> *"The mobilization station will inspect the deployment packets for each soldier to ensure that all soldier readiness processing (SRP) tasks were completed to standard prior to mobilization. Only those tasks that were not completed or were not properly documented will be executed at the mobilization station.*
>
> *The focus of training for mobilizing units will be to achieve all established training requirements and to ensure that soldiers are properly prepared, both mentally and physically for combat. If a unit can document that training tasks were conducted to standard prior to arrival at the mobilization station, there is no requirement to execute these tasks again. (Most installation Commanders at various Mobilization Stations throughout the United States try to) capitalize on tasks conducted prior to arrival at the mobilization station by using (their) training resources to bring the unit to an even higher state of training readiness prior to deployment. Ultimately, (the) goal (of the Mobilization Station) must be to deploy only those soldiers and units that have met all established criteria for deployment. (It is the Commander of 1st Army intent to)*

hold mobilization station(s) and training support brigade commanders responsible to ensure every soldier is fully trained and equipped prior to deployment, and (1st Army reserves) approval authority for any exceptions from this policy." [10]

In my case, the unit I was mobilized with was sent to Ft. McCoy, Wisconsin. "Fort McCoy is a Total Force Training Center with a mission to enhance readiness by supporting training, serving as a Power-Projection Platform for mobilization and providing installation-management expertise. Soldiers training at Fort McCoy have access to a full spectrum of facilities, ranges, training areas and classrooms that support individual and collective training compatible with environmental standards. The installation also features an air-to-ground impact area and airborne drop zones for both personnel and equipment. A state-of-the-art Multi-Purpose Training Range permits armor, mechanized infantry and combat aviation units to conduct annual crew qualification. Recent additions to training facilities include an Urban Training Complex, a Combat Pistol Qualification Range, a Modified Record Fire Range and a Multi-Purpose Machine Gun Range. The Fort McCoy complex is situated on 60,000 acres, 46,000 of which are available for maneuver training. More than 60,000 additional acres are available in neighboring counties through training land-use agreements."[11]

Global War on Terror

Fort McCoy has supported many national defense missions, including Operations Iraqi Freedom, Enduring Freedom and Noble Eagle. More than 71,000 military personnel from 47 states and two territories mobilized or demobilized at Fort McCoy since Sept. 11, 2001.[12]

Upon arrival at your mobilization station, it is imperative that that you understand that the mobilization station processing is a very thorough and detailed process. The biggest piece of advice that I would give a deploying service member is to ensure that they keep track of all the records and documents that they receive, not only during the mobilization station process but throughout the time of their deployment. These documents will be necessary if there is ever a need to verify information in the future. The following details much of what you will encounter at your mobilization station for processing, as well as some tips to make the process run as smoothly as possible.

Tom and friend LTC Howard.

Mobilization Station Processing

Upon arrival at the mobilization station, you will be accessed onto Active Duty and undergo standardized processing consisting of medical and dental screening, input to the Army's pay and personnel systems, security clearance validation/initiation,

ID card and ID tags, uniform issue, and other administrative actions. This process takes approximately three days. To facilitate your inprocessing, please bring any prior military records in your possession, such as your military personnel file, immunization records, service documents such as DD214's or NGB22's (documenting prior military service), medical/dental records, or immunization records. Always retain a duplicate copy of important service documents for your records and provide copies to HRC-STL. These copies will be included in your permanent official file. (NOTE: If you are found medically or otherwise non-deployable during the mobilization process, you may be released from active duty.)

Tom preparing for the rifle range.

LNO/Installation Team Support

At the mobilization station, you will be processed and cared for by a team consisting of Liaison Officers (LNOs) from the Army's Human Resources Command (HRC) St. Louis and your host installation. Address any questions, concerns, or issues that you may have to these individuals. They are there to support you and make your inprocessing as smooth as possible. Behind this team is an extensive support network of training, pay and personnel specialists extending from the reception battalion at the installation level all the way up to Headquarters, Department of the Army. If the HRC-STL LNO team is not physically located at your mobilization site during your inprocessing, and you need additional assistance, call HRC-STL's Mobilization Hot Line toll free at 1-800-325-4361 or commercial 314-592-0559.

Warrior Task Training

Following your administrative processing, you will receive 7-10 days of Warrior Task Training (WTT) in basic Soldier skills including weapons qualification, NBC training, first aid, and law of land warfare.

Additional MOS/AOC Training

Upon validation of WTT, depending on your individual situation and training status, you will then attend either approximately three weeks of military occupational specialty (MOS)/area of concentration (AOC) refresher training or MOS reclassification training (proponent school). The MOS/AOC specific training may be provided at a different installation from where your inprocessing and WTT occurred. Therefore, you may be required to transfer to another installation for follow-on training.

Unit Assignment Instructions

Just prior to the completion of training, your assignment instructions will be finalized and forwarded on to the installation commander who will then publish temporary change of station (TCS) orders to transfer you to your eventual place of duty/unit of assignment. The intent is to link you up with your designated unit at the mobilization station for collective training with the unit prior to deployment. (Efforts will be made) to link you up with your final unit of assignment as soon as practicable. Remember, your final assignment will be made based upon the needs of the Army.

Expected Processing/Training Period

Your full processing and training may take approximately 2-3 months prior to your deployment. During your administrative inprocessing and follow-on training, despite the Army's best efforts, you may experience delays and encounter changes along the way as a result of real world considerations. Sometimes your projected unit of assignment or MOS specialty requirements for a given unit may change. Thus, your final assignment may be adjusted due to changing operational priorities or circumstances, which may arise beyond the Army's control. (Please be) understanding if changes occur.

(The Mobilization Station's) Commitment to You

Remember always that you are not alone. ...HRC-St. Louis LNO teams, along with your host installation support team, are committed to serving you in every possible way. LNO teams will be there to help you resolve any issues that you may encounter during your tour of active duty. You are the reason they exist. Realize also that the mobilization station is there to ensure support and assistance to you does not end upon your assignment to a unit. They are committed to supporting you throughout your mobilization, deployment, and redeployment home in any manner possible.

Keep Document Copies/Provide to HRC-STL

As previously mentioned, it is imperative that you keep copies of all documents provided to you while on active duty and provide copies of the following documents to HRC-STL. These documents include but are not limited to:

1. ALL orders (to include any amendments).
2. Servicemembers Group Life Insurance (SGLI).
3. NCO Evaluation Reports/Officer Evaluation Reports.
4. Awards and decorations.
5. DD Form 214 (and DD 215, DD220, if issued).
6. NGB Form 22 (documenting National Guard service).

HRC-STL also HIGHLY recommends that you take a separation physical at the end of your tour. This will be very important should you encounter any medical issues in the future that may be related to this deployment.

Communication is Key

(For example) All Soldiers are required to establish Army Knowledge Online (AKO) email accounts prior to mobilization/deployment at the following website: www.us.army.mil/portal/portal-home.JHTML AKO is rapidly becoming the Army's primary means of communication/interface with

Soldiers. Therefore, you will be severely handicapped if you do not have an active AKO account. Your AKO email account is an essential lifeline between you and the Army, as well as between you and your family during your mobilization. The HRC-STL support team will also communicate with you during your active duty tenure through your AKO email account. (HRC-STL) stand(s) ready to assist you in resolving any issues that you or your family has. However, (they) also need your help and cooperation in keeping the lines of communication open by notifying us as soon as possible of any important changes or issues that you face throughout your mobilization.[13]

MAKING THE MOST OF YOUR TIME DURING MOBILIZATION

Despite all the very good training I received during the two months that I was at my mobilization station, I found that I had a great deal of "down time". I have spoken to hundreds of deployed service members and the consensus is that the time spent at the mobilization station can and should be shortened. Many service members have told me that they were bored and restless. While I strongly believe in being prepared to go to war, there comes a point of diminishing returns and you just end up wasting time and resources that could better be used for something else.

If you are a Commander and want to use the time spent at your mobilization station wisely, I would suggest to the extent possible, you identify to a degree of certainty what specific jobs your service members will do once they arrive in theater and train them as they would fight. The "kitchen sink" approach to training is not only a waste of time but a poor use of valuable resources during the time of war. It was during my mobilization station time that I learned what my first assignment for the first year of what would turn into a 2-year combat deployment would be. I was appointed as the Deputy Chief for Theater Rest and Recuperation or R&R. With this knowledge, I was able to communicate with the outgoing Deputy and learned a great deal of what I would be doing prior to even arriving in Kuwait.

One of the biggest pieces of advice I would like to share with a deploying service member is to use the time you spend at the Mobilization Station to get your "head in the game"! You will be away from home for a year or more and it may be the first extended absence for you and /or your young children.

While at my mobilization station, I made certain covenants with myself. The first half of 2006 was a very stressful time in my life both personally and professionally. In addition to those conditions, my health was getting worse. At the time I reported to my unit for deployment in support of Operation Iraqi Freedom, I weighed 316lbs and had a waist size of 54 inches. I made a commitment that during the time I was at my mobilization station I would get into shape as well as develop a healthy life style. I also endeavored to get spiritually stronger. One way I would accomplish this was by reading the book by Rick Warren entitled *Purpose Driven Life*. By the way *Purpose Driven Life* has been one of the best books I have read to date.

The book has helped me in all areas of my life.

As with any journey short or long, it begins with the first step. My first step both with deciding on a healthier life style and becoming spiritually stronger began with my decision to live a better life... A PURPOSE DRIVEN LIFE! From there my verbal plans were placed into action. I started to change the way I ate. I also started walking everywhere and turning down rides with my fellow service members even if it meant me walking for 20 minutes instead of taking a 3-minute vehicle ride. These little steps would soon pay big dividends after arriving at my war time duty station in the Iraq war theater of operations.

Determine your "purpose" for the next six months, one year, or however long you will be deployed. What do you hope to accomplish for yourself personally? Physical fitness, spiritual awakening, or educational achievements? Plan for how you will strive to accomplish these goals during your deployment. Start planning during the time you spend at the mobilization station. Identify gym facilities or educational course offerings that will be available to you at your deployment location. Believe me, a clear plan for improving aspects of your life while deployed, and actually implementing that plan, will make you a better person once you return from deployment.

It is important to keep in mind that generally prior to departing for your overseas tour, you will be provided an opportunity to go home on what is termed a "4 day pass." A pass is different from leave in so much as the service member is not "charged" for the days taken. It is in effect non-chargeable time off. This is your last opportunity to spend time with your family and friends prior to actually departing for your assignment and duty station overseas. So use the time wisely! For me, my 4 day pass was during the time of the Michigan State Fair. So it was a great time to have fun with my wife Trina, daughter Marissa and son Troy. They truly loved it. Taking me to the airport after my 4 day pass was a very sad time for the family. I did not return home until nearly 6 months later.... It was now time to go to war!

PART 3
A Time of New Beginnings!

Tom on a camel in Kuwait.

September 9th, 2006 was the start of something new. That was the day that I arrived in Kuwait to start what would turn out to be the first of my two combat deployments in the Middle East! I remember that day very well. I had just left Wisconsin where temperatures were a cold and rainy 40 degrees, flew over to Iceland where there was a refueling stop and continued on stopping again in Germany and then on to Kuwait where we landed at Kuwait City International Airport (KCIA), the military side.

When the door of the aircraft opened, it was well over 113 degrees. The heat took my breath away. If only I had known then what I know now, I would have realized that 113 was cool. I have seen days in Kuwait were the temperature never dropped below 130 degrees for days on end. The temperature on several occasions flirted with 150-degrees. I should also point out that at night, temperatures in the summer time would only get

On the way to Kuwait City

down to a relatively cool 105 degrees!

Prior to leaving for Kuwait it was determined that my duty location would be with Coalition Forces Land Component Command (CFLCC). The name was latter changed to United States Army Central Command or USARCENT, headquarters on Camp Arifjan, Kuwait. Kuwait is a remarkable country. The massive growth of the petroleum industry transformed Kuwait into one of the richest countries in the Arabian Peninsula and by 1952, the country became the largest exporter of oil in the Persian Gulf. This massive growth attracted many foreign workers, especially from Egypt and India. Kuwait settled its boundary disputes with Saudi Arabia and agreed on sharing equally the neutral zone's petroleum reserves, onshore and offshore. After a brief stand-off over boundary issues, Iraq formally recognized Kuwait's independence and its borders in October 1963. During the 1970s, the Kuwaiti government nationalized the Kuwait Oil Company, ending its partnership with Gulf Oil and British Petroleum. In 1982, Kuwait experienced a major economic crisis after the Souk Al-Manaka stock market crash.

Kuwait had heavily funded Iraq's eight yearlong war with Iran. By the time the war ended, Kuwait decided not to forgive Iraq's US$ 65 billion debt. An economic warfare between the two countries followed after Kuwait increased its oil production by 40 percent. Tensions between the two countries increased after Iraq alleged that Kuwait was slant drilling oil from its share of the Rumaila field. On 2 August, 1990 Iraqi forces invaded and annexed Kuwait. Saddam Hussein, then President of Iraq, deposed the emir of Kuwait, Jaber Al-Sabah, and installed Ali Hassan al-Majid as the new governor of Kuwait. After a series of failed diplomatic negotiations, the United States-led coalition of thirty-four nations fought the Persian Gulf War to remove the Iraqi forces from Kuwait. The coalition successfully liberated Kuwait from Iraqi occupation on February 26, 1991. Kuwait paid the coalition forces US$17 billion for their war efforts.

During their retreat, the Iraqi armed forces carried out a scorched earth policy by damaging 700 oil wells in Kuwait, of which approximately 600 were set on fire. It was estimated that by the time Kuwait was liberated from Iraqi occupation, about 5 to 6 million barrels (950,000 m^3) of oil was being burned in a single day because of these fires. Oil and soot accumulation had affected the entire Persian Gulf region and large oil lakes were created holding approximately 25 to 50 million barrels (7,900,000 m³) of oil and covering 5% of Kuwait's land area. In total, about 11 million barrels (1,700,000 m³) of oil was released into the Persian Gulf and an additional 2% of Kuwait's 96 billion barrels (15,300,000,000 m³) of crude oil reserves were burned by the time the oil fires were brought under control. The fires took more than nine months to extinguish fully and it took Kuwait more than 2 years and US$50 billion in infrastructure reconstruction to reach pre-invasion oil output. Kuwait has since largely recovered from the socio-economic, environmental, and public health effects of the Gulf war.[14]

I recommend to all serve members, as soon as you learn where you will be deploying to, do some research about the country you will be living in. You may actually learn something new. More importantly, you will be better prepared to serve your country as well as interact with the local population. You should also know that you will be required to attend cultural awareness classes prior to arriving in country.

Regardless of whether you are deploying to Iraq, Kuwait, Afghanistan, Qatar, Djibouti or anywhere in the world for that matter, doing your research ahead of time will pay big dividends upon your arrival. You may even get a leg up on learning the local language, customs and courtesies.

Despite having just traveled some 8 thousand miles over a period of two days. Despite not having had a shower. Despite not having slept and being extremely tired, the first thing that you will do upon arriving in country is "swipe" into theater. This is a process whereby your identification card is scanned and most of your identifiable data is downloaded into a system. This is done for several reasons. The first and foremost reason is for accountability, and the second reason being that is how finance knows to start your entitlements. Your entitlements include among others items your combat pay, hazardous duty pay, overseas pay and separation allowances. Also, the fact that you are in a combat zone entitles you to receive federal tax-exempt status on all your military earnings. As such, you do not pay taxes on your "base" pay. There is a cap on the amount of your base pay that is exempt from taxation. Once you reach your cap, you will have to pay taxes on all earnings over that amount. However, most service members regardless of rank will benefit from it. The only question is what amount of your base pay will be tax exempt. I would encourage service members to contact their finance office for more details.

For service members whose final destination is Iraq or Afghanistan, they spend a few weeks in Kuwait at Camp Beuhring. Camp Beuhring is an amazing facility. The camp itself was named after LTC Chad Beuhring who was killed in a rocket attack on a hotel he was staying in while in Iraq. Camp Buehring is approximately 8 miles in circumference, self sufficient and contained.

Camp Beuhring

Everything from water to food to fuel is trucked in daily to support the soldiers that train just prior to being sent to Iraq and Afghanistan.

Tom in a Kuwait City hotel.

Camp Buehring could rival some US bases. A fully-stocked exchange, several phone centers, an internet café, a coffee house, gym facilities, Burger King and a 24-hour Pizza Inn are just a few of the amenities here topping the service members' "favorites list."[15]

RIP/TOA

Now that you have arrived in theater and know where you will work, you are probably wondering what happens next? Regardless of where you end up, prior to jumping into your job, you will go through what is referred to as a RIP/TOA. RIP/TOA stands for Relieve in Place and Transfer of Authority. It is the sequence of events where one military unit replaces another in a theater or area of operations. This is an opportunity for the outgoing unit to train their back-fill. Usually what happens during this time is the outgoing unit personnel will continue doing their job while the new unit personnel sit next to the outgoing personnel. This is done for about a week. Subsequently, the new unit service members will then take over and the outgoing personnel will ensure the job is being done correctly. This is also referred to as the "right seat/left seat" ride which is part of the RIP/TOA process. It is said that this phrase has its origins in drivers education were the student driver and instructor sit side by side.

Once the right seat/left seat training is completed there is generally a ceremony referred to as the Transfer of Authority or TOA. This basically means the new unit personnel have assumed all responsibilities and duties of the outgoing unit personnel.

Kuwait Towers, rebuilt after heavy damage in the Gulf War.

Kuwait Deployments v Iraq Deployments

There seems to be a great debate among the service members that are deployed in support of Operations Iraqi Freedom and Enduring Freedom. The debate centers around the belief by those serving in Iraq and Afghanistan that service members serving in Kuwait are less deserving of Rest and Recuperation Leave and that their service is less dangerous and thus not worthy of receiving all the benefits of those serving in a combat zone. (Despite the fact that service in Kuwait is considered service in a combat zone!)

The fact of the matter is, those serving in Kuwait, Qatar and other locations in the region but outside of Iraq and Afghanistan are just as vulnerable to being attacked and killed as those service members serving in Iraq and Afghanistan. Those serving in Kuwait may get a false sense of security, as they are not being shot at daily. But all must recognize that all countries in the region, including Kuwait, Iraq, Saudi Arabia, Iran and Qatar (home to the me-

Tom at the Giant Pearl, a Qatar landmark.

dia conglomerate Al Jazeera) have extremists living within their borders that would love to do serious harm to the American way of life as well as kill service members.

The bottom line is, never let anyone tell you that you are less of a combat soldier and not deserving to wear the combat patch nor receive the benefits of being in a combat zone. The truth of the matter is we are all in this war on terrorism together and the war in Iraq could not succeed without the support and service of those serving in Kuwait as well as others around the world.

Moreover, we are all away from family, friends and love ones and regardless of where you serve you feel the separation.

Taking Advantage of Special Benefits While Deployed

There are many financial and other benefits that service members have as a result of their deployment in the combat zone. As discussed earlier, they will receive certain tax benefits as well as additional money due to their service in a combat zone. There are also various savings and investment programs that should be considered as well as quality of life issues that are determinative of were you are stationed.

Financial Benefits

There are many benefits that service members have as a result of their deployment, which will vary depending on whether you are deployed to a combat zone. As mentioned earlier, you

Tom flying over Iraq.

will receive certain tax benefits as well as additional money due to service in a combat zone. There are also various savings and investment programs that should be considered.

A Breakdown of your Pay While Deployed[16]

Hardship Duty Pay-Location (HDP-L): Enlisted and officers deployed in an area designated by the Secretary of Defense as HDPL, are entitled to HDP-L. This entitlement is payable on a daily basis, begins on the day of arrival in country, and stops the day of departure. Rates are $50.00, $100.00, or $150.00 and are based on location. The entitlement starts on the 31st day and is retroactive to the first day of eligibility.

Family Separation Allowance (FSA)

Married Soldiers and single Soldiers with primary physical custody of a child are entitled to FSA-T when separated from their dependents for more than 30 days. A member married to another member with no dependents is entitled to FSA, provided the couple resided together prior to the deployment (only one member is entitled if both are deployed). FSA is payable at $250 per month ($8.33 per day). It begins the day of departure from home station, and ends the day prior to arrival at the home station (DD 1561). The entitlement starts on the 31st day of separation and is retroactive to the first day of eligibility. Remember, the servicemember must be separated more then 30 consecutive days before the entitlement kicks in. FSA stops the day prior to arrival at home station.

Hostile Fire/Imminent Danger Pay (HF/IDP)

This entitlement begins the day of arrival and ends the month of departure from a designated HFP location. HF/IDP is payable at $225 a month. Soldiers present for duty in any of the designated areas for one day during the month are authorized the entire $225 for that month.

Combat Zone Tax Exclusion (CZTE)

All enlisted Soldiers and warrant officers present for duty in any of the designated areas for one or more days are exempt from federal and states taxes for the entire month. Commissioned officers are also exempt from federal and states tax, limited to the maximum enlisted pay per month (the SMA base pay plus $225 for HFP/IDP). At the time of writing this book, the servicemembers' base pay is exempt from Federal Income Tax, up to $6,724.50 per month. NOTE: Soldiers have 180 days after redeployment to file federal income taxes. Write "OEF/OIF from (start date) to (end date)" at the top of your return to avoid a late fee or penalty.

Basic Allowance for Subsistence (BAS)

BAS continues for all Soldiers receiving this allowance prior to deployment. Soldiers receiving partial BAS at their permanent duty station will be authorized BAS for the length of their deployment. BAS is payable at $267.18 per month for enlisted members, and $183.99 for officers.

BAS will not change for the period of deployment. If you received rations in kind no available (or RNA) prior to deployment, your BAS will not change for the period of deployment. If you are designated as Essential Station Messing or Meal Card Holder, your collection will stop for the period of deployment. When you return to home station, your BAS will revert back to your pre-deployment amount.

Basic Allowance for Housing (BAH)

A Service member's BAH is based on his/her duty station. Moving dependents while deployed will not change BAH. For example, if a soldier is stationed at Fort Benning, their BAH stays at Fort Benning's rate even if the Servicemember elects to move dependents. Servicemembers receiving BAH without dependents can elect to store household goods (HHG) at the government's expense or at their own expense and retain the BAH without dependants. Soldiers assigned to single-type quarters continue receiving partial BAH.

Reenlistment Bonus

If a reenlistment contract awarding a bonus is signed while in a CZTE area, the bonus and anniversary payments are exempt from federal tax. Anniversary payments for a reenlistment signed outside a CZTE area remain taxable even if paid in the CZTE area. Leave sold by an enlisted member in the CZTE area, whether earned in that area or not, is tax exempt.

Special Leave Accrual (SLA)

SLA allows Service members to carry forward up to 90 days of leave at the end of the fiscal year (60 days ordinary leave plus 30 days special leave accrual). USAREUR units may submit unit's requests for SLA. Refer to AR 600-8-10.

MY PAY

This convenient online resource allows you to record and print out pay changes to your federal tax, direct deposit, a leave and earnings statement (LES), address, TSP, allotments, and bonds. It also allows you to you set up a restricted access PIN for significant others. For more information go to https://mypay.dfas.mil.

It is important to note that if a spouse has a general power of attorney, he/she can get an LES or a W2. If they have a special power of

Tom on the firing range.

attorney with it stating they can stop, start, or change allotments, he/she will be able to do that. They can also initiate contributions to the savings deposit program by starting an allotment or a cash contribution.

SAVINGS AND INVESTMENT PROGRAMS

TSP

The first plan I will discuss that is offered by the government to servicemembers is known as the Thrift Savings Plan. The Federal Thrift Savings Plan, or TSP, is a retirement savings plan for civilian employees of the federal government and members of the military. The TSP closely resembles an employer's 401(k) plan. Military members are generally not eligible for matching contributions received by civilians.

The TSP offers the same type of savings and tax benefits that many private companies offer their employees.[17]

Savings Deposit Program

This savings/investment plan is primarily available to deployed servicemembers. While the TSP is available to everyone in the military. The Savings Deposit Program (SDP) is available only to those serving in designated combat zones. Military members deployed in combat zones, qualified hazardous duty areas, or certain contingency operations may deposit all or part of their unallotted pay into a DOD savings account up to $10,000 during a single deployment. Interest accrues on the account at an annual rate of 10% (per Executive Order 11298) and compounds quarterly. Although federal income earned in hazardous duty zones is tax-free, interest accrued on earnings deposited into the SDP is taxable. Members can designate the allotment amount in five-dollar increments.

Eligibility

Eligibility to participate in the SDP depends on where the service member is stationed and the type of service. The service member must be receiving hostile fire/imminent danger pay, and be serving in a designated combat zone or in direct support of a combat zone for more than 30 consecutive days or for at least one day for each of three consecutive months. Designated SDP areas remain designated until the Undersecretary of Defense withdraws the designation or until the areas' designation for imminent danger pay terminates, whichever is first. Current SDP services designations are as follows:

- ★ Effective 2 August 1990, members serving in the Persian Gulf Conflict to include the Arabian Peninsula to include the Persian Gulf (as defined by the Arabian Peninsula, the Strait of Hormuz, and that part of the Gulf of Oman which lies north of 25 degrees north latitude and 057-30 degrees east longitude), Bahrain, Iraq, Iran, Israel, Jordan, Kyrgyzstan, Kuwait, Lebanon, Oman, Pakistan, Qatar, Saudi Arabia, Tajikistan, Turkey, United Arab Emirates, Uzbekistan, and Yemen.

- Effective 1 January 1996, members serving in Operation Joint Endeavor to include the Bosnia-Herzegovina, Croatia, Serbia, Montenegro, Slovenia, Macedonia, Hungary, and the air space thereof, or the waters of the Adriatic Sea of North of 40 degrees North, plus forces operational control/tactical control to Supreme Allied Commander, EUROPE for the purpose of executing Operation Joint Endeavor.

- Effective 1 January 1997, members serving in Operation Joint Guard and, effective 20 June 1998, members serving in Operation Joint Forge to include the total land area of Bosnia-Herzegovina, Croatia, Serbia, Montenegro, Slovenia, Macedonia, Hungary, and the airspace thereof, or the waters of the Adriatic Sea north of 40 degrees North.

- Effective 1 November 2001, members serving in Operation Enduring Freedom to include the total land area of Afghanistan, Pakistan, Kazakhstan, Kyrgyzstan, Qatar, Tajikistan, Turkmenistan, United Arab Emirates, and Uzbekistan. The waters of the red sea, the gulf of Oman, and the Arabian Sea (portion north of 10 degrees North latitude and 68 degrees East longitude) or in the airspace thereof.

★ Effective 1 February 2003, members serving in Operation Enduring Freedom\Iraqi Freedom to include the total land area of the Arabian Peninsula to include the Persian Gulf (as defined by the Arabian Peninsula, the Strait of Hormuz, and that part of the Gulf of Oman which lies north of 25 degrees north latitude and 057-30 degrees east longitude), Bahrain, Iraq, Iran, Israel, Jordan, Kyrgyzstan, Kuwait, Lebanon, Oman, Pakistan, Qatar, Saudi Arabia, Tajikistan, Turkey, United Arab Emirates, Uzbekistan, and Yemen.

Making a Deposit

Service members may begin making deposits on their 31st consecutive day in the designated area. Eligibility to make deposits terminates on the date of departure from theater. Active duty members may make deposits by cash, personal check, traveler's check, money order or allotment. Reserve component members may make deposits by cash, personal check or money order only. Standing policies regarding personal check acceptance and regulatory restrictions regarding number and type of allotments apply.

All deposit amounts, regardless of depository method, must be made in $5 increments (e.g. $50, $65, $1005, not $1001.67), and cannot exceed a service member's monthly-unallotted current pay and allowances (e.g. monthly net pay after all deductions and allotments; includes special pays and reenlistment bonus). More than one deposit via cash, personal check, traveler's check, or money order may be made in a month but the cumulative total of the deposits cannot exceed the month's unallotted pay and allowances.[18]

For up-to-date information on the Savings Deposit Program you should contact your finance office. It is important to keep in mind that service members must stop their allotment to the SDP program when they redeploy; the allotment will not stop automatically.

You are also advised to keep a copy of all Cash Collection Vouchers or (DD Forms 1131) you receive from your deposit. I can tell you from first hand experience that but for my records of all deposits made, I would have been short over $1,000.00 that the administrators of the program lost track of.

It is also important to note that interest stops 90 days after redeployment; therefore, it is recommended that you withdraw funds no later than 90 days after redeployment. To request your money, you should write to DFAS-CL, ATTN: Code FMCS, 1240 E 9th Street, Cleveland, OH 44199-2055 to withdraw your deposited money. Be sure to also include in your letter: Name, SSN, branch, bank routing number, account number or address for check, separation date, and date of departure from the deployed area. Include with the letter a copy of all cash collection vouchers DD Forms 1131.

Regardless of your desire to participate in these savings plans, I strongly encourage everyone to participate in the Savings Deposit Program. To not do so would be foolish. There is no reason to turn down a guaranteed rate of return of 10%. Such a rate of return beats the stock market in many cases.

Alpha party in Kuwait.

REST AND RECUPERATION

Rest and Recuperation or R&R is something that all service members look forward to receiving while deployed. Most importantly, R&R is an opportunity for you to see and spend time with family and loved ones. It is also an opportunity to decompress away from the battlefield.

On 25 Sep 03, USCENTCOM initiated an R&R Leave Program for all service members, Active or Reserve, and DOD civilian employees assigned to a 12-month tour of duty to one of 17 designated contingency countries within the USCENTCOM AOR in support of Operation Enduring Freedom or Operation Iraqi Freedom. The seventeen countries designated for R&R eligibility are Afghanistan, Bahrain, Djibouti, Iraq, Jordan, Kuwait, Kyrgyzstan, Oman, Pakistan, Qatar, Saudi Arabia, Somalia, Syria, Tajikistan, Uzbekistan,

United Arab Emirates, and Yemen.

The final decision regarding eligibility rests with the commander within theater and is based upon the following factors: (1) Mission. The commander may determine that mission constraints require the restriction of R&R leave. (2) Personnel strength. No more than 10 percent of the force within theater can be on leave at one time. (3) Re-deployment activities. In some cases, personnel assigned to units scheduled to re-deploy to their home stations within 90 days may not be able to take R&R leave.

Although many personnel may be eligible for R&R leave, not every eligible member will be able to take R&R leave due to mission constraints, personnel strength, or redeployment activities.[19]

The U.S. Army Central Command (USCENTCOM) Rest and Recuperation (R&R) Leave Program provides 15 days of chargeable leave to service members and Department of Defense (DOD) Civilians who are deployed on one-year tours to contingency locations within the USCENTCOM area of responsibility in support of Operations Iraqi Freedom and Enduring Freedom. The program provides fully funded travel from Kuwait City International Airport to the commercial airport nearest the participants' final leave destinations worldwide. The program operates flights 365 days a year. Effective July 13, 2007, service members and DOD Civilians deployed on 15-month tours were authorized 18 days of chargeable leave, and the unit personnel absence ceiling was raised to provide as many service members and Civilians as possible with the opportunity to participate.

"Congress and DOD senior leadership recognize that R&R opportunities are vital to maintaining combat readiness and capability for units deployed and engaged in intense, continuous operations. It promotes increased operational effectiveness by mitigating the effects of prolonged combat stress and Family separation." [20]

R&R participants who choose to travel to foreign countries for their R&R leave are responsible for complying with those countries' requirements regarding passports and visas. Refer to the Foreign Clearance Guide for specific country requirements. The website for the Foreign Clearance Guide is https://www.fcg.pentagon.mil/fcg.cfm.

Tom with professional sheep herders.

R & R Passes

Service members are not authorized to take R&R Leave within the first 60 days of "boats on ground," unless an exception is granted. However, an individual can use an R & R Pass at any time.

The R&R Pass is a program that allows for service members to take a 4-day pass to Qatar to decompress from the stress of war. Another important difference to note is that R&R pass leaves are not chargeable against accrued annual leave. In other words, the time you are away on pass will not count against you for leave days. Something to consider if you want to use your R&R Leave days as terminal leave. More on terminal leave later in the book.

A service member is allowed to take a 4-day pass for every 6 months "boats on the ground." However unlike R&R Leave, the service member does not have to wait 60 days to take their 4 day pass. They can in fact take their pass after spending 1 day in country, though I cannot imagine why you would need to use the pass so early on. It is important to know that this is an option.

Qatar is a fascinating place to visit. Of course there is a wide variety shopping in the capital of Doha. Open markets (sougs) offer everything imaginable from clothing, electronics and perfume oils. Soug Waqif is the oldest market and is place to buy meal, wool and other staples. Other sougs specialize in gold and household goods. Be prepared to bargain as everything is negotiable! City Centre Doha is the largest shopping complex in the Middle East and offers many familiar retail brands as well as independent stores.

Tom in Doha, on the banks of the Persian Gulf.

I personally enjoyed shopping for jewelry like salt-water pearls while in Qatar. You will see many jewels that are not readily available in other parts of the world.

You might also consider taking a sand dune adventure. Tour guides are available to transport you up and down 60-metre dunes where you will have an unparalleled view of the desert. A lunch and swim in the warm inland sea will nicely top off your adventure before you make the journey back to the city. Be sure to bring swimsuit, sunscreen, and don't forget your camera. For a desert safari, choose a reputable ground tour operator. Excursions should be undertaken in an adequately-equipped 4 x 4 vehicle. Always travel in convoy with other cars, take a supply of water, a mobile telephone if you have one, and be sure that at least one other person is aware of your plans.[21]

Regardless of weather you are taking R&R Leave or the 4 day R&R Pass, you should be mindful that unless an exception to policy is approved, no more than 10% of your unit can be on leave at any one time. This 10% rule includes service members on R&R Leave, R&R PASS, Emergency Leave as well as any other absences. Be as flexible as possible when requesting your leave dates, although most Commands are sensitive to life events that can not be recaptured such as a child's graduation from school.

The USO

The United Services Organization or USO is known as a service member's home away from home. During my travels both as a deployed service member on active duty and as a part time Army Reservist, I have found the USO to be an Oasis of calm in the middle of my hectic travels.

According to the USO's own website,

> "The USO is a private, nonprofit organization whose mission is to support the troops by providing morale, welfare and recreation-type services to our men and women in uniform. The original intent of Congress — and enduring style of USO delivery — is to represent the American

Tom with cast members from "The Unit."

people by extending a touch of home to the military. The USO currently operates more than 130 centers worldwide, including ten mobile canteens located in the continental United States and overseas. Overseas centers are located in Germany, Italy, the United Arab Emirates, Japan, Qatar, Korea, Iraq, Afghanistan, Guam, and Kuwait. Service members and their families visit USO centers more than 5.3 million times each year. The USO is the way the American public supports the troops."

During my combat deployment I worked closely with the USO in Kuwait. Among the entertainers and celebrities that visited soldiers included world-renowned golfers such as Tom Watson and Butch Harmen as well as movie stars Scarlett Johansson and actors from the Unit, The Terminator and the hit TV show 24, comedians, cheerleaders, and music groups.

Additionally there are USOs throughout the country that serve as rest stops for service members at airports around the country. While returning from my two-year combat deployment, I stayed over night at the USO located at the Chicago airport and was treated like royalty. Most important it did not cost me a dime. I was also provided with more food then I could eat, a phone card to make phone calls home, use of a computer, gym and television with more cable channels for me to remember. If you find yourself with some down time at an airport or stranded, you would be advised to visit the local USO.

For more information about the USO check out their website at: www.uso.org.

1. Puddle of Mudd
2. Tom & Pussy Cat Doll Nicole Scherzinger
3. Tom & Wesley Reid Scantlin, Puddle of Mudd
4. Tom & Solonitics
5. Carlos Mencia with Tom

1. DJ Ztrip & Tom
2. Tom with actress Scarlett Johansson
3. Tom with Twista and crew
4. Twista in concert

1. Comedian Vince Morris & Tom
2. Tom Watson & Tom
3. Race car driver Erica Enders & Tom
4. Racing Heroes: Jeremy Mayfield, Erica Enders, (Tom) Clay Millican, Phil Burkart
5. Tom and Hype Man

1. Disturbed
2. Disturbed & Tom
3. Washington Redskins Cheerleaders

1. Tom Backstage
2. Tom & American Idol, Bo Bice
3. Tom & Sheryl Underwood (Comedian)
4. NFL two-time Pro bowl & Superbowl XXXV Mike McCrary with Tom

5. Coaches: Dave Leitao, Gary Steward, Ed Conroy, (Tom), Jeff Nix, Jim Crews, Jeff Bzdelik

1.

2.

3.

4.

1. Tom & Myspace Tom
2. Pro golfers: Tom Lehman, Butch Harmon, David Feherty, (Tom) Tom Watson, Joe Inman, Howard Twitty
3. Dallas Cowboy Cheerleaders
4. Actor Gary Senise with Tom

DEPARTMENT OF THE ARMY

THIS IS TO CERTIFY THAT THE SECRETARY OF THE ARMY HAS AWARDED

THE ARMY COMMENDATION MEDAL

TO

CAPTAIN THOMAS A. MENGESHA
UNITED STATES ARMY CENTRAL

FOR MERITORIOUS SERVICE IN SUPPORT OF OPERATIONS IRAQI AND ENDURING FREEDOM WHILE SERVING AS THE DEPUTY FOR THE THEATER REST AND RECUPERATION PROGRAM. HE WAS RESPONSIBLE FOR MANAGING FORTY MILLION DOLLARS IN GOVERNMENT CREDIT CARD ACCOUNTS WITH 100 PERCENT ACCURACY. HIS LEADERSHIP AND ATTENTION TO DETAIL WERE INSTRUMENTAL IN ORCHESTRATING THE 500,000 PASSENGER MILESTONE CELEBRATION. CAPTAIN MENGESHA'S DISTINCTIVE ACCOMPLISHMENTS REFLECT GREAT CREDIT UPON HIM, THE COMMAND, AND THE UNITED STATES ARMY.

FROM: 10 SEPTEMBER 2006 TO 30 AUGUST 2007

THIS 3rd DAY OF JULY 2007

PO 184-3, 3 July 2007
United States Army Central
Camp Arifjan, Kuwait

R. STEVEN WHITCOMB
Lieutenant General, US Army
Commanding General

DEPARTMENT OF THE ARMY

THIS IS TO CERTIFY THAT THE SECRETARY OF THE ARMY HAS AWARDED

THE ARMY COMMENDATION MEDAL

TO

CAPTAIN THOMAS A. MENGESHA
BASE SUPPORT BATTALION-NORTH

FOR MERITORIOUS SERVICE WHILE ASSIGNED AS THE ADJUTANT IN SUPPORT OF OPERATION IRAQI FREEDOM. HIS DEDICATED SERVICE WAS KEY IN THE SUCCESSFUL ACCOMPLISHMENT OF MORALE, WELFARE AND RECREATION EVENTS AS WELL AS VIP VISITS AT CAMP BUEHRING. HIS PERFORMANCE OF DUTY AND DEDICATION TO SOLDIER READINESS REFLECTS GREAT CREDIT UPON HIM, AREA SUPPORT GROUP-KUWAIT AND THE UNITED STATES ARMY.

FROM: 1 SEPTEMBER 2007   TO: 5 JULY 2008

THIS 24TH DAY OF AUGUST 2008

PO 237-1, 24 Aug 08
Area Support Group-Kuwait
APO AE 09366

CHRISTOPHER K. HOFFMAN
Colonel, AR
Commanding

Tom with Secretary for Homeland Security for The United States of America, Michael Chertoff

BECOMING A U.S. CITIZEN

Becoming a United States Citizen is a dream for many. There are additional benefits to becoming a United States Citizen while deployed. For one thing, the process is faster than the average applicant who is not in the United States Military. Moreover, there are no costs associated with the process if you apply for citizenship while deployed in a combat war zone.

If you are a member of the U.S. Armed Forces and are interested in becoming a U.S. citizen, you may be eligible to apply for citizenship under special provisions provided for in the Immigration and Nationality Act (INA).

The INA has been revised to make it easier for individuals serving in the military to become United States citizens. Normally, a non-citizen wishing to become a United States Citizen must have five years of legal permanent residency in the U.S. to apply. Non-citizens married to a U.S. citizen for at least three years can apply after three years of residency.

For members of the Armed Forces the following apply:

Peacetime Military Service

Under INA Section 328, persons who have served in the U.S. Armed Forces (including active duty, reserves, or national guard), can file for Naturalization based on their current or prior U.S. military service.

The requirements for eligibility are that the applicant must have served honorably or have separated from the service under honorable conditions, have completed one year or more of military service, and be a legal permanent resident at the time of his or her examination by USCIS on the Form N-400, Application for Naturalization.

Service During Hostilities

By Executive Order Number 13269, dated July 3, 2002, President Bush declared that all those persons serving honorably in active-duty status in the Armed Forces of the United States at any time on or after September 11, 2001 until a date to be announced, are eligible to apply for naturalization in accordance with the service during hostilities statutory exception in Section 329 of the INA to the naturalization requirements. This means that individuals with even one day of honorable active duty service can apply for citizenship, regardless of how long they have been a resident.

Posthumous Citizenship

Under section 329a of the INA, non-citizen servicemembers who die while serving honorably in an active-duty status during a declared period of hostilities, including Operation Enduring Freedom, and Operation Iraqi Freedom, and whose death was as a result of injury or disease incurred in or aggravated by that service, are eligible for posthumous naturalization. An application for posthumous citizenship can be filed on behalf of the deceased servicemember only by the next-of-kin or another representative. If the application is approved, the individual is declared a U.S. citizen retroactively to the day of his or her death.

Section 319(d) of the INA provides for the naturalization of the surviving spouse of a U.S. citizen who died while serving honorably in an active duty status in the armed forces of the United States. The spouse and U.S. citizen service member must have been living in marital union at the time of the citizen's death. All the other usual requirements for naturalization must be satisfied except that no prior residency or physical presence in the United States, a state, or immigration district is required to file a naturalization application.

Every military installation should have a designated point-of-contact to handle your application and certify your Request for certification of Military or Naval Service (N-426). You should inquire through your chain of command to find out who this person is, so that you can help you with your application packet.

The Department of the Army has directed its Battalion (BN) and Brigade Combat Team (BCT) S-1s, Personnel Services Battalions (PSB), Personnel Service Centers (PSC), Military Personnel Divisions (MPD), and Military Personnel Offices (MILPO) to assist Soldiers with their applications for citizenship and to coordinate with the U.S. Army Human Resources Command (USAHRC) as necessary to facilitate the process.

The Air Force has designated Military Personnel Flights (MPFs) as their functional area for citizenships. Airmen can also complete applications online through the virtual Military Personnel Flight.

For the Navy, each Naval command is required by NAVADMIN 251/04 to establish a Citizenship Representative.

The Designated Representative for the Marine Corps is the

servicing Legal Assistance Officer, according to JAL Advisory #16.²²

MAKING THE MOST OF YOUR TIME DURING DEPLOYMENT

Regardless of your duty location, I recommend that you make the most of your time in your new controlled environment. You can begin implementing the development plan you made while at the mobilization station. How you spend your time will be determined by the location and mission you have.

For example, service members stationed in Qatar may have greater freedoms then say someone in Kuwait. Service members in Kuwait will have greater freedoms then service members in Iraq and Afghanistan. However, one thing is certain; you will have some free time. How you use it can pay big dividends to you in the future.

Tom's Thanksgiving meal.

While I was deployed to Kuwait I focused on myself and what I wanted to change about myself. As I indicated earlier in this book, when I was mobilized I weighed in excess of 316lbs and had a 54-inch waist. Getting in shape was a major goal I had. At the end of my deployment I had dropped approximately 100lbs and reduced my waist size to 38 inches. This took sacrifice and commitment. There are many misconceptions about military food, however, one thing is certain, while you are in a deployed environment on a major military installation lack of food will never be a problem! In addition you will be exposed to no less than 4 "feedings" per day and all the cake and ice cream you desire. It takes a disciplined person who is committed to losing weight to avoid falling into the trap of gaining weight.

In my case I decided to work out everyday (7 days a week) in addition to cutting out deserts and candy. I used the elliptical for 1 hour and 5 minutes set at level 12 and I would follow that up with about 15 minutes of abs work. Additionally, I would incorporate weight resistance training into my daily routine. As seen by these photos, the results speak for themselves.

After failing the Army Physical Fitness Test or APFT every year for 5 years, I finally passed on December 6, 2006. I did so well on my APFT that my Commander thought I cheated on the test and ordered me to take it again two days later. Despite my dissatisfaction I complied, and two days later I scored even higher the second time! This gave me a tremendous sense of pride. To this day, that has been one of my most cherished memories in the military.

The point I want to make is that you should not think of this time as a curse; but remember the phrase "if life gives you lemons, make lemonade!" My deployment was a stressful time, however, I used the time to make lemonade.

Depending on the amount of time and or special skills you have, being deployed can produce an opportunity for you to make additional money. I know of several service members that used their deployment to make some extra cash. Here is how.

Tom "Before" in September 2006 (above), and "After," a year later, in September 2007 (right).

Most military installations have sporting events and are in need of referees. Morale Welfare and Recreation or MWR will pay a service member for each game they officiate. In my case, once word got around that I was an attorney, I was offered several teaching opportunities. In May of 2007 I was hired to teach Business Law at the University of Maryland University College as an instructor. In September of the same year, I was granted the rank of Adjunct Assistant Professor earning over $2,000.00 per 8 week class. Not bad for a part time gig. I would encourage all of you to look into teaching opportunities. It is important to note, that while the extra money was nice to have, keeping myself busy also helped to make the time go by faster and made dealing with being away from home a little easier.

Tom with Business Law students from
University of Maryland Uuniversity College

Cards, Letters, Gifts, and Care Packages

When it comes to receiving mail, there is no group of people in the world that appreciate the receipt of a letter or package more so than service members in a deployed environment. Even if you are receiving mail and care packages from home, there is no such thing as too much letters and packages from the home front. There are many organizations that sponsor deployed service members for the purpose of sending cards, letters and packages, or providing services to them and their families. A number of these organizations solicit the help of individuals and companies willing to support the military by sponsoring a service member. The list below is an example of the support available:

> **4theTroops**—Coordinates the shipments of supplies, goods and gifts to our service members abroad.
>
> **The Billy Blanks Foundation**—The Billy Blanks Foundation was founded by the creator of Tae Bo. One of the foundations many projects is sending care packages to U.S. Service members in Iraq and Afghanistan.
>
> **Christmas for Troops**—Paying Tribute to our Military Troops During the Holidays.
>
> **Adopt a Platoon**—Support the troops through gifts and sponsored mail.

Any Soldier—Sponsor care packages to service members in Iraq.

Blue Star Mothers—Organizes postcards to troops and care packages, and is currently petitioning Congress for reduced air fares for servicemembers.

Books for Soldiers—Donate books, movies, and more.

A Million Thanks—Collects emails and letters of appreciation for our armed forces.

Operation Gratitude—Contribute to care packages sent to our servicemembers.

Operation Homefront Hugs—Contribute to care packages, or adopt a servicemember.

Operation Military Pride—Sends letters, care packages, and gifts overseas.

Operation USO Care Package—Sponsor a care package for $25. Contribute to care packages to be sent overseas—www.SupportUSTroops.com

Voices From Home—Voices From Home allows serving military members and their families and friends to send and receive immediate voice e-mail messages.

America Supports You

"America Supports You," a nationwide program launched by the Department of Defense, recognizes citizens' support for our military men and women and communicates that support to members of our Armed Forces at home and abroad. All across America, thousands of individual citizens, businesses, and groups—from local schools and establishments to nationally-known corporations and organizations—host events and undertake projects to support America's Armed Forces, especially in forward-deployed areas of the Global War on Terrorism. Military members can access the web and learn about America's support for their service. For more information on the program visit www.AmericaSupportsYou.com.[23]

Subscriptions for Service Members

Another great program for deployed service members is known as the Subscription for Service Members program. This program allows your family, friends, or supporters to send you a magazine subscription as a way of giving thanks. Any overseas active duty Service Member in the Army, Navy, Air Force or Marines can take part in this program at no cost to you. Register at: http://subs4servicemembers.com/ .

Regarding the organizations that specialize in sending care packages to soldiers, I would recommend registering with one or more of these programs as soon as you know your duty location and address. I am certain that once an organization "adopts" you, you will receive something in the mail to pick your spirits up.

Now that you have reached your deployed destination, assumed the duties of your job (whatever it may be), decided on what areas of your life you want to improve on and signed up with various organizations to receive cards, letters and care packages, it is now a time for new beginnings!

LESSONS LEARNED

CRISP Yard

From souvenirs to additional equipment, it is surprising just how much "stuff" service members acquire during their deployment. Most service members, after spending a year in a deployed environment, will accumulate a tremendous amount of property. I was surprised at how much "stuff" I had acquired after only being in Kuwait for 1 year. It should then come as no surprise that after spending two years in the desert, I pretty much amassed a small museum of artifacts and items that I had picked up along my travels throughout the Middle East.

One issue that often arises among service members deals with shipping personnel property back home. The answer is not as simple as one might think. We are all aware of the U.S. Postal Service, however, service members may pay hundreds of dollars to ship their items home. There is another avenue to ship your personnel property home that costs nothing.

The Central Receiving and Shipping Point or "CRSP Yard" as it has come to be known in some circles is a great opportunity for service members to ship large amounts of personnel property home at no cost. The items are not actually sent to your home but to a military center closest to your home. From there, you must retrieve the packages yourself.

You may ask yourself why do this when all you may want to do is put everything in your unit designated "conex"? That may be an option; however, most unit conexs have to be packed for shipment as much as 45 days prior to the unit departing from theater. Most importantly not all deployed service members will return to the home station of the unit they deployed with.

For example, as I previously mentioned, when I was deployed in 2006, I was considered an Individual Augmentee (IA). My Reserve Unit was a unit in Michigan but my deploying unit, with whom I had no previous relationship, was in South Carolina. Sending my personnel items in the Unit conex of the South Carolina unit would have made no sense as I live in Michigan and that is where I would be returning. Also, the unit I deployed with left a year prior to my redeployment in 2008.

Shipping my property through the Central Shipping and Receiving Point or "CRSP Yard" was the perfect choice for me. However, it is important to point out that you will still have restrictions on items sent in the mail in much the same way as you would if you shipped them at the post office. For example, you will not be able to mail back hazardous material, weapons, or classified material in most cases.

Arrangements may have to be made for customs agents to inspect your shipment prior to mailing. However, if you are willing to undergo a few minor inconveniences, the "CRSP Yard" may be the way to go when shipping personnel property home.

Voting while deployed

It occurred to me during the presidential campaign of 2008 that I was witnessing history in the making. For the first time in American presidential politics, all the major candidates were Senators. For the first time in the history of American politics, an African American and a former prisoner of war (POW) all had a real and viable chance of being elected President of the most powerful country in the world, The United States of America. In fact, on November 4th, 2008 history was made! As it turned out, the young (47 years old) and energetic Senator from Illinois won the election by a large margin. Senator Barack Obama beat out Senator John McCain and was elected as the 44th President of The United States of America on a message of change. In addition to becoming the nation's first African American President, President Obama became every service members' Commander-in-Chef of the most powerful military in the world.

Congressman Brad Ellsworth & Tom

Yes-siry that was a very exciting time for me indeed! After all, I have always been a political conesore. In December of

2007, I completed an extensive certification training program and was certified by the Department of Defense Federal Voting Assistance Program as a Voting Assistance Officer (VAO). As the VAO, I was responsible for providing accurate, non-partisan voting information and assistance to service members and others wanting to exercise their Constitutional right to vote.

Voting is more then just a constitutional right it is also a privilege that should not be taken for granted. Many have fought and died to give individuals around the world the opportunity to take part in democracy. Voting is the great equalizer. Your vote matters and your vote counts! It matters not how much money you have, your position in society or your birth lineage, all votes count the same.

For example, the President's vote carries the same weight as the homeless town bum living on the street. Bill Gates' vote carries the same weight as the single mother on welfare with 5 children to feed. That is the beauty of our electoral system in America. While you are deployed, you should not give up your right, your duty to vote. You should and must vote!

You may be asking yourself how I can vote when I am deployed and serving in Iraq, Afghanistan, Kuwait or anywhere outside of the United States for that matter? The answer is simple. Obtain an absentee ballot. With an absentee ballot you will be able to write in your candidate of choice and have your vote counted as though you never left the comforts of home. It is important to contact your individual state for greater details on the voting process as every state has their own election roles. A good starting point to get information may be found at http://www.fvap.gov/index.html

Service Members and their Political Activities

It seems that for as long as I can remember, I have been fascinated with politics. As a child growing up on Pawley's Island South Carolina, I was one of those rare children that would enjoy watching the news as well as Sunday morning talk shows. Even to this day when I want to relax, I will sit down in front of the television and watch a good talk/news program. If I have to take a long road trip I will listen to talk radio over a music station any day. However, doing this drives my daughter Marissa crazy as she is a huge Hannah Montana and Keyshia Cole fan.

I do not know were this fascination with news, information and politics came from but for what ever reason; it is at the core of who I am. Maybe it came from a recorded sermon by Dr. Martin Luther King Jr. I heard as a child. As I recall the name of Dr. King's sermon was "The Drum Major Instinct". That sermon affects me to this day. If you ever get a chance to read it in it's entirety you should but it would be even better if you heard the words as spoken by Dr. King. The following is just a small part of that sermon.

> "...And so Jesus gave us a new norm of greatness. If you want to be important—wonderful. If you want to be recognized—wonderful. If you want to be great—wonderful. But recognize that he who is greatest among you shall be your servant. That's a new definition of greatness. And this morning, the thing that I like about it: by giving that definition of greatness, it means that everybody can be great, because everybody can serve. You don't have to have a college degree to serve. You don't have to make

your subject and your verb agree to serve. You don't have to know about Plato and Aristotle to serve.

You don't have to know Einstein's theory of relativity to serve. You don't have to know the second theory of thermodynamics in physics to serve. You only need a heart full of grace, a soul generated by love. And you can be that servant..." (www.stanford.edu/group/King/publications/sermons/680204.000_Drum_Major_Instinct.html)

While a student in college at The University of South Carolina, I ran for several political offices. These offices ranged from being appointed as Chief Student Advocate to running for student Senator, as well as my failed but valiant attempt at becoming student body President. I actually did pretty well considering I was considered the new kid on the block and was out spent by my opponents. You would be surprised at what some of those kids spent to run for office. You would have thought we were trying to run for President of the United States.

I remember

Congresswoman Sheila Jackson Lee & Tom

campaigning like I was running for President of the United States. In fact, I coined the phrase "State of the University Address". When asked about some of the changes I would bring into office if elected, I responded that I would give weekly State of the University Addresses to keep the students informed about the goings-on on campus. To this day, I am proud I came up with that phrase.

However, when it comes to political activities while in uniform, service members must think twice. I have been involved with many election campaigns over the years from local, state and federal elections but while wearing the uniform there are certain types of activities that I, nor any other service member, can undertake.

In short, while in uniform, a service member can not carry on certain types of political activities. Types of activates forbidden while in uniform include, but are certainly not limited to, attending rallies, using government vehicles or conducting political activities while working, using their military influence to interfere with the election process as well as speaking before a partisan political gathering, including any gathering that promotes a partisan political party, candidate, or cause.

I should also point out that as an officer serving in the military, it is a violation of the Uniform Code of Military Justice or UCMJ to speak out against the President. I remember a case of a military General that made some disparaging remarks about then President Clinton. After those remarks came to light the general was forced to resign.

However, you are allowed to speak as a private citizen and of course while not in uniform about a particular candidate you would like to support. You can give money to the candidate just as any private citizen can do. According to the Department of Defense Directive 1344.10, you may also "attend partisan and nonpartisan political fundraising activities, meetings, rallies, debates, conventions, or activities as a spectator when not in uniform and when no inference or appearance of official sponsorship, approval, or endorsement can reasonably be drawn." Remember, you must not be in uniform! For more information relating to the Department of Defense Directive 1344.10 which relates to political activities by members of the armed forces visit: www.dtic.mil/whs/directives/corres/pdf/134410p.pdf

Nevada Governor, Jim Gibbons & Tom

★   ★   ★

Fear none of those things which thou shalt suffer: behold, the devil shall cast [some] of you into prison, that ye may be tried; and ye shall have tribulation ten days: be thou faithful unto death, and I will give thee a crown of life. (Rev 2:10)

PRISONER OF WAR

I have never been officially declared a Prisoner of War or POW but I have been detained against my will. Being a prisoner of war must certainly be one of the most terrifying conditions a service member must face. Most foreign POWs are mistreated and certainly (in most cases) not treated as well as POW's held by the United States. As a POW, expect to be held in conditions that are trying both mentally and physically. You may be confined and restrained to a very small area and have your movements strictly controlled. You should also understand that even as a POW, you have a Code of Conduct that must be followed.

The Code of Conduct is the legal guide for the behavior of military members who are captured by hostile forces. The code itself is broken down into six Articles that address various situations that may arise. The military Code of Conduct is as follows:

Article I

I am an American, fighting in the forces which guard my country and our way of life. I am prepared to give my life in their defense.

Article II

I will never surrender of my own free will. If in command, I will never surrender the members of my command while they still have the means to resist.

Article III

If I am captured I will continue to resist by all means available. I will make every effort to escape and to aid others to escape. I will accept neither parole nor special favors from the enemy.

Article IV

If I become a prisoner of war, I will keep faith with my fellow prisoners. I will give no information or take part in any action which might be harmful to my comrades. If I am senior, I will take command. If not, I will obey the lawful orders of those appointed over me and will back them up in every way.

Article V

When questioned, should I become a prisoner of war, I am required to give name, rank, service number, and date of birth. I will evade answering further questions to the utmost of my ability. I will make no oral or written statements disloyal to my country and its allies or harmful to their cause.

Article VI

I will never forget that I am an American, fighting for freedom, responsible for my actions, and dedicated to the principles which made my country free. I will trust in my God and in the United States of America.

As a POW, you may become sad, depressed and even suffer from anxiety attacks, but you must always keep your wits about you! You may be confined and even separated from other prisoners, and you may not know what the future holds. Always know that there are people and forces out there that are trying to reach you and set you free. The military will never abandon one of its own!

If you find yourself a Prisoner of War or detainee, the following are some things that may help you as they helped me through my ordeal as a detainee.

1. Start a routine or an activity to keep your mind off your current condition and circumstances.
2. Exercise. Even in a confined environment, you can do activities to stay in shape.
3. To the extent possible eat as best you can, there are certain foods that have stress lowering properties. According to some nutrition experts, foods that help fight anxiety are:

    a. Berries, any berries

    b. Guacamole

    c. Mixed nuts

    d. Oranges

    e. Asparagus

    f. Chai tea

Understand as a POW you will only be able to eat what is offered, but at least now you have an idea of some good food choices.

5. Get as much fresh air as possible. Every opportunity you have should be a chance to take in some fresh air. When I was a detainee, I suffered an anxiety attack like non other I had suffered before. What helped me was taking in as much fresh air as possible.

6. If there are other POW's at your facility it may be helpful to build relationships. The company of others is a good thing during stressful times. When I was a detainee, I shared a small space with another detainee named Anthony Wright from Chicago. While we had extremely different backgrounds, we both did a lot to keep each other's spirits up. We would tell each other jokes and share the limited supplies our detainers provided us. Anthony Wright helped me survive my ordeal as a detainee and for that, I am eternally grateful.

Lastly, you should never give up hope. You should pray to whatever power gives you strength as well as spiritual renewal. The power of prayer is real and should not be taken lightly or for granted. Remember your training. Remember you are not alone. Remember they may have your body but never your mind! Remember that your family, friends and country love you and will never forget you. Keep the faith. Pray and most of all, always remember that God will be with you...always!

BATTLEFIELD STRESS

Whether you wear a medal on your chest or just courage in your heart, the effects of war are real. Service members should never be ashamed to seek mental health counseling. There is no shame in recognizing that you are having problems dealing with the effects of your combat deployment. In fact, it is honorable and shows a great deal of courage for you to seek out and get the treatment you need to succeed. In the past seeking mental health counseling may have affected your ability to obtain or keep a security clearance or even certain jobs in the military. Recently there have been changes on security clearance application procedures. You are now allowed to check the "no" block when asked if you have any mental health issues as long as you are seeking and undergoing treatment with a mental health provider.

As I look back over the two years I spent deployed to the Iraq war theater of operations, I am amazed at the many experiences I have had. I have held positions that helped service members return home for much needed Rest and Recuperation as the Deputy Chief of USARCENT's R&R Program. The R&R program, with nearly a billion dollar per year budget, did just that. I also, on a more relevant note to this book, held the position of S1/Adjutant. However by the end of my deployment I learned that the truly most important thing in life was the connection you have with family and friends. Family is and will always be the most important thing in my life. My wife has surprised me with her strength and courage. Remember when you serve, your entire family serves with you. When you are under stress so is your family. It took a combat deployment for some to realize this fact.

If you suffer from stress associated with your deployment contact your base mental health provider or the Veterans Administration. They are well equipped to assist you as you navigate on your road to recovery and mental health bliss.

DEATH

What happens if you or a loved one dies in a combat zone? Once the word got out that I was a licensed attorney in the state of Michigan it seemed that I was appointed to any assignment that remotely dealt with law, investigations or legal matters. One such appointment dealt with being selected and appointed as a Casualty Officer. That required attendance at a week long training seminar located at Camp Arifjan, Kuwait where I learned the ins and outs of notifying family members of the death of service members and information about the death benefits that are provided to the surviving family. During my deployment, I was assigned to investigate the death of a soldier and make a "line of duty" or LOD determination as to the cause of death. My investigation could have resulted in a recommendation that the deceased service member did not die "in the line of duty" and as such was not entitled to death benefits afforded to service members who are killed or die while serving. My findings could have resulted in the non-payment of hundreds of thousands of dollars to the surviving family. However, as a result of my investigation, I recommended and my recommendation was accepted that death benefits should be paid to the service member's beneficiary.

So what happens if you die while serving in a combat zone? Well, if you prepared adequately, your loved ones will be better prepared to move on with their lives. One of the first things you should be aware of is that within 72 hours of your death in a combat zone your family will receive a check sent via electronic funds transfer to their bank account in the amount of $100,000. That money should be used to take care of the survivors' affairs until the Service Member's Group Life Insurance or SGLI is paid, which usually takes place within 30 days. Unless otherwise selected, the policy will pay $400,000. (This amount is in addition to the $100,000 already received in the first 72 hours following the death). In addition to the money paid to the beneficiary or beneficiaries, there are additional entitlements that will be paid upon your death. The Casualty Assistance Officer assigned to the family will provide all the details.

Upon your death, your next of kin must be notified within 24 hours of your death. The notification is made by someone of the same or higher rank and usually that person is accompanied by a Chaplin. The sole purpose of the notification is to inform the next of kin and let them know that a family Casualty Assistance Officer will be appointed to assist with the rest of the process as well as explain the benefits available to assist the family.

As it relates to the cause of death, there will be no speculation given. The lessons learned from the death of famed football player turned soldier Pat Tillman are many. Pat Tillman was killed in Afghanistan by friendly fire. However, much of the information put out early on was wrong and some have even claimed that it was intentionally distorted to make the military look good.

What happens to personal affects of the deceased service member?
With regard to property, you should know that all of your property will be inventoried and shipped to the next of kin. A little known fact; if you have a computer, that computer will first be shipped to a location were it will be scanned for anything that may be offensive to the next of kin, such as a spouse. The purpose for this is simple. If something like a love letter to anyone other than the spouse is discovered, that letter will be deleted from the system to protect all concerned parties.

IMPROVE YOUR FOXHOLE

Although your deployment may seem like an eternity, it is not. Whatever job, duty or responsibility you have, you should always find ways to improve your "foxhole." What is meant by improving your "foxhole?" The term foxhole, also referred to as "a defensive fighting position (DFP), is one of several types of earthwork constructed in a military context. Each stage develops the fighting position, gradually increasing its effectiveness, while always maintaining functionality. In this way a soldier can improve the position over time, while being able to stop at any time and use the position in a fight."[24]

Relating this to your job in the deployed environment means that at all times you should be coming up with ways to make your job better for the next person that will have to do it. Your job is your "foxhole." Improving the way it is done will only make the war effort stronger and success more certain.

As the S1/Adjutant, I developed a comprehensive protocol policy that dealt with VIP and other Distinguished visitors that visited troops in the war zone. I had the privilege of escorting and briefing many political leaders and celebrities while servicing in my position as Adjutant for Base Support Battalion-North.

Lazar Elenovski, Macedonia's Minister of Defense with Tom

Financial Liability Investigation of Property Lost (FLIPL)

One would be amazed at just how many hats an Adjutant wears in the course of any given day. One such hat I wore on several occasions was that of an Investigator. I investigated a wide range of issues such as investigations of solders accused of disrespecting a Non Commission Officer (NCO). Another case involved the cause of death of a service member which required me to make a recommendation as to whether or not his death was in the "line of duty." However, the most tedious types of investigations I was appointed to investigate dealt with the loss of government property by service personnel.

It is mind boggling to know that every year tens of thousands if not millions of dollars worth of property go unaccounted for in military inventories. I have found that the typical situation involves poor accountability of government property and rarely does it involve theft of government property. However someone will have to pay for the lost, misplaced or damaged property, and typically it is the person who signed for the property.

I would advise any service member, be they a Commander or Private, to ensure that they properly account for all property that they signed for. And while it may be time consuming and tedious, if you loan out property that you signed for, ensure that the person who takes the property from you signs for the property. You want to always ensure the property is signed for down to the user level. NO EXCEPTIONS!

If you find yourself the target of a Financial Liability Investigation of Property Loss or "FLIPL" remember some important basic points. First, if you have properly kept accurate records of all property you are responsible for, you will have little to worry about. This includes ensuring your hand receipts are up to date and all property is sub-hand receipted down to the user level. NO EXCEPTIONS!

You will generally have 30 days to contest the findings of the FLIPL investigator and will even be given the opportunity to speak with an attorney. After the 35th day has passed, the recommendation and findings of the FLIPL Investigator will go to the approving authority for action, which may include recoupment of all or a portion of the value of what has been lost.

When taking the loss value of the property into consideration, the FLIPL Investigating Officer can reduce the amount of loss via the concept known as depreciation. There are formulas used to do this, however, one such formula will allow for the reduction of lost property value due to depreciation by up to 25%.

One final point to remember is that in most cases, the actual amount of loss to be recovered from the "Respondent" is limited by their base pay. So for example, if "Respondent" losses 2 million dollars worth of property, the most they would have to pay would be up to one month of their base pay and for the average service member that would be less than $4,500.00 per month.

For more information on the role of the FLIPL Investigator and what to expect if you are the subject of an investigation, check out the Department of the Army Pamphlet 735-5, "Financial Liability Officer's Guide" at: www.army.mil/usapa/epubs/pdf/p735_5.pdf.

PART 4
"POP SMOKE!"

Tom standing with the unit crest for 3rd PERSCOM (FWD) at camp Arifjan, Kuwait.

Before you realize it, it will be time to "pop smoke" and start the processes of redeploying back home. The phrase "pop smoke" is an old infantryman term. When an infantryman decides to make a strategic exit from combat, he will "pop smoke." However in this case, you pop smoke when the mission is complete. In civilian life, "popping smoke" describes the act of making a strategic exit from any situation. I like this phrase because it communicates an abrupt and final act that indicates your desire to leave the area, stop what you are doing, or just go home!

DCS Briefing

Approximately 60 days from your departure out of the war zone you will attend several briefings. A short but very important step in the process of returning home, the DCS briefing is short for Deployment Cycle Support. While this briefing may seem boring and a waste of time. You will do well to pay very close attention to the information presented at the briefing.

Among the topics that will be discussed include preparing financial matters. Family support issues will also be discussed. This is usually accomplished with the aid of a Chaplin.

Travel Vouchers

Relating to financial matters, there have been estimates that thousands of service members regardless of whether they deployed with a unit or were individual augmentes as I was, have lost hundreds if not thousands of dollars in entitlements by way of travel voucher settlements.

The finance portion of the briefing is usually presented by a representative of the finance office on camp. The biggest issue that is continually brought up and I must admit even I was surprised, was the lack of service members that complete the necessary paperwork to receive their travel entitlements. While the service member is entitled to certain funds that fall under travel pay, if they do not complete the necessary paperwork, they will never receive these funds. It has been estimated that thousands of service members forego receiving travel pay that amounts to hundreds if not thousands of dollars per person. Most service members' travel settlement payment is in excess of $1,000.00 and for those service member that have been deployed continually for over 2 years, they can expect to receive approximately $3,000.00 in travel funds. However, I can not emphasize enough the importance of completing the necessary paper work to receive the money.

You may be wondering how travel pay is determined.

Travel pay primarily consists of a daily rate of per diem. Effective 1 October 2003, each Soldier is entitled to receive a daily incidental per diem of $3.50/day OCONUS or $3.00/day CONUS. Soldiers will receive the entire per diem once they complete a final travel settlement voucher (DD Form 1351-2) at their home station upon re-deployment. ALL travel vouchers MUST be submitted with orders and reviewer's signature; if not, it will be returned.

One of the last things you will do prior to leaving your deployed position is to ensure that continuity is maintained. One way this is accomplished is conducting a RIP/TOA. Much like what happened when you first arrived, you will now be in the position of training your replacement to assume the duties that you and your unit have been performing over the past 12 to 15 months.

Some advice for those preparing to start the process is to ensure that once contact is made with your replacement, you provide them with as much information as possible to make the transition as smooth as possible. For example, there may be some online training that could be taken care of while the newly deploying personnel are at their mobilization site. There are safety classes as well as drivers training and other courses that should be taken care of prior to being deployed to the war zone. Waiting to take these courses will only "eat away" the amount of time you could be spending to learn your job when you arrive in theater.

Once you meet your replacements, it is best to find out their strengths and weaknesses. Doing so will prevent the wasting of time, "spinning" the service member up in areas they are already familiar with and could probably teach you a thing or two about.

Another point to keep in mind is, mail as many things as you possibly can back home before you leave so that you do not have to carry it. You will be surprised how much "stuff" you will accumulate during your period of deployment.

I will make a statement about war trophies. Souvenirs can be an important and memorable way to document your experiences while deployed to the war zone, however, if you intend to bring home war trophies please be advised that in most cases it is illegal. However, due to recent and continual changes in law, I would advise you to speak with your local military legal counsel. There are some items that can be brought back home. You want to ensure that your items are returned via legitimate as well as legal means.

It should be noted that all letter size mail sent from a military APO back to the states are FREE to mail! That is right. It cost nothing to mail a letter from your deployed area. You just have to write FREE MAIL in the upper right hand corner where the stamp would have been placed. I am certain I saved a hundred dollars in postage because of this benefit.

It is now time to Pop Smoke!

Tom with actress & model Leeann Tweeden.

PART 5
MISSION ACCOMPLISHED

SGT Lakesha S. McNeil celebrates the news of returning home!

Arrival at your demobilization station may bring mixed emotions. On the one hand you are very excited about going home to see loved ones yet on the other hand you may be a little apprehensive about how the people in your life have changed, as well as how you have changed. I will never forget the words of another service member, SGT Lakesha S. McNeil from Jackson, Mississippi prior to departing for my first deployment. She indicated that no mater who you are, you will certainly be affected by your combat deployment experience. If I ever run into Lakesha in the future, I will let her know that she was right.

Upon my arrival at Ft McCoy Wisconsin, my demobilization station, I was eager to get my demobilization process underway. Service members returning from a combat deployment must undergo thorough records check and medical evaluations to ensure that not only their records are in order, but their mind and body are well and prepared to be reintroduced to civilian life.

I found this process to be very well organized and easily navigable. The process of demobilization consists of several stations. In my case, I was considered an Individual Re-deployer. That meant that I did not have to navigate the demobilization process with a large unit. Instead, I was able to just slide in where I could get in! Expecting to spend as much as a week or more at the demobilization station, I actually spent less than 3 days there. I have heard horror stories of service members spending weeks at their respective demobilization stations. Often times the reason for the delay is classified as a "medical holdover." Medical holdovers are service members that may have contracted an illness or disease that prevented them from being reintroduced back into society. One such example of this is contracting Tuberculosis, a highly contagious disease. Another example would be in the case of the service member that needed to have emergency surgery.

Among the stations that each service member must process and clear prior to being released from active duty include the following:

1. Audiology
2. Record Review
3. Chaplain
4. Legal
5. Dental

6. Retention

7. Medical

8. LODs

9. ACAP

10. Finance

11. DD214

12. ID Card

13. QA Survey

14. Final SRC Checkout

No matter how much preparation one does in preparing to deploy, I am amazed at how important things get missed. For example, as I processed through the ID Card station, I learned that I was never coded as someone serving on "Contingency Operations" duty. In a nut shell, that meant that if someone in the future questioned whether I had ever served in support of Operation Iraqi Freedom, much less served in Kuwait, I could have been denied certain benefits that are only available to those who serve under that coding. I certainly would have had to jump through hoops to prove I was eligible for those benefits.

I have some very important advice for those National Guardsmen and Reservists out there. If you have built up leave days, it is imperative that you depart theater in enough time so that you do not lose those days. The exception would be if you fall into a certain category, such as having served in Iraq or Afghanistan, with the hopes of taking advantage of the Post

Mobilization Respite Absence or PDMRA benefit program.

PDMRA is a program designed to offer benefits to those service members who served in Iraq and Afghanistan without being able to utilize their accrued time off with the family. The Secretary of Defense directed the implementation of a program to compensate individuals who are required to deploy or activate within establish dwell time. This incentive is to be in the form of "administrative absence".

If for example a Reservist or National Guard service member serves two consecutive tours, they would be offered additional non-chargeable leave days. They would not lose those days even if they did not have available days to take them. Instead, what would happen is that upon reaching their demobilization station, their orders would be extended giving them the opportunity to take their leave without the loss of their benefits and entitlements. If you arrive at your demobilization station with more leave days then days left on your orders, you could lose those accrued leave days.

Consider the following. Service Member "A" departs Kuwait with 10 days left on his orders but has 30 days of accrued leave. Upon arriving at the demobilization station, he would be able to use up to 10 days of transitional leave and would be required to sell back the remaining 20 days.

Why is that important you might ask? Well when Service Member "A" sells back his 20 leave days, he will lose his "day for day" credit for his retirement calculation, which may cause a possible reduction in retirement benefits. Additionally, he will lose his housing allowance payment for those days which could amount to over $1,000.

Now consider Service Member "B". She departs Qatar with 35 days left on her orders but has 30 days of chargeable leave. Upon arrival at her demobilization station, she would be able to take her entire 30 days of leave plus earn her day for day credit for retirement purposes. In addition, she would also continue receiving her housing allowance. Service Member "B" is a much happier and wealthier service member.

However, you can avoid the pitfalls of Service Member "A" by just ensuring you depart theater with enough time to utilize all of your earned chargeable leave. There are exceptions to this such as obtaining a letter from an O6 in your chain of command. However, you must plan ahead. Remember YOU are the only one that is responsible for your career!

It cannot be stressed enough how important it is to keep copies of records in your file and ensure that your file is correct and updated! Without over exaggerating, I went through no less than four Soldier Readiness Processes or SRPs prior to mobilization in support of Operation Iraqi Freedom. However, during my demobilization phase after my two years of active duty, it was discovered that my records were not coded correctly and not giving me credit for serving in contingency operations. So in fact there was not a record of me serving in a war zone. How could this happen you might ask? Well I will respond by telling you what the fine young woman told me as I passed through her "ID Card" section; "If it is not THEIR records, no one cares." In other words, you are the best custodian of your career and your records. No one else will put as much time and effort into ensuring your files are up to date as you!

REUNITING WITH FAMILY

Experts say that it can take anywhere from 6 to 18 months to return to "normalcy" after a combat deployment. I can tell you that the relationships you maintained and possibly improved upon will shorten that time. For many the first emotion felt after coming home from a combat deployment may be surprising. Things to look for upon a service member's return from a combat deployment and how to react are as follows:

1. The returning Service Member may have moments of isolation.

2. They may also have high emotions.

3. You as the family member should listen but do not react to the service member's possible expressions of anger.

4. However, you should never accept emotional or physical abuse.

It has been said that war is hell! However with proper planning you as well as your family and other relationships will survive. It is very important to take your time and expect a readjustment period. You have been gone away from home for a very long time. This absence is only compounded if you have small children. When I left home my son was 9 months old and upon my return he was nearly 3 years old. I saw a tremendous growth. There was an adjustment that we both made. Even though you may not notice, you and your loved ones have changed in many ways. Take it slow and seek help if needed from your local family support center or religious/spiritual advisor. Do not let your marriage, friendships or any other positive relationship become a casualty of war.

POST-DEPLOYMENT RESOURCES AND SUPPORT

Outward Bound Wilderness Excursions for Operations Enduring and Iraqi Freedom Veterans

After spending time in a combat zone you will certainly need some time to relax and unwind. One program designed to do just that is the Outward Bound Wilderness Excursions for OEF/OIF Veterans. Outward Bound is an international non-profit outdoor education program which is offering fully funded outdoor adventure excursions to all OEF/OIF veterans. It doesn't matter what your current military status is—you're eligible to attend as long as you deployed in support of OEF/OIF combat operations while in the military.

These five-day excursions offer adventure activities such as backpacking, rock climbing, canyoneering, canoeing, and dog sledding in beautiful wilderness areas. Past locations have included Maine, Texas, Colorado, California, and Minnesota.

All expedition costs for lodging, equipment, food, and instruction are completely funded by a milt-million dollar Sierra Club grant, including the participants' round-trip transportation between home and the wilderness site. That is right, these excursions are offered at no cost to the participant!

For more information pertaining to the Outward Bound OEF/OIF War Veterans Expeditions check out their website at www.OutwardBoundWilderness.org/veterans/html

Transition, Scholarships and Vocation Rehabilitation

These organizations provide transitions services, scholarships and vocational programs to help service members and their families re-integrate into the civilian world.

> **The Billy Blanks Foundation**—The Billy Blanks Foundation was founded by the creator of Tae Bo. The foundation offers scholarships and support for after school programs.
>
> **The Freedom Alliance**—Organizes donations and contributions for our servicemembers, and also awards scholarships.
>
> **Operation One Family**—Helps provide life skills, education and continuing support for the families of our fallen military heroes.
>
> **Sacred Heart Lodge**—Provides a cost free hassle free vacation to those Soldier's who are returning from War to reconnect to their Families.
>
> **Soldiers' Angels**—Support group aids wounded Soldiers with transitional backpacks, personal visits, and phone calls, etc., and also

sends thanks via letters and email to the U.S. military and its allies.

Counseling and Other Relief and Support Organizations

The following organizations provide a wide range of services and support for our troops and wounded veterans including counseling, financial support, housing, emergency services and more:

> **Air Force Aid Society**—Official support and relief organization for Air Force service members, veterans, and families
>
> **The Armed Forces Foundation**—Provides support and educational help to our troops.
>
> **Armed Forces Relief Trust**—Combination of the major military relief societies takes donations to help service members
>
> **Army Emergency Relief**—Official support and relief organization for Army service members, veterans, and families.
>
> **CarePages.com**—Offers opportunities for wounded warriors and their families to post prayer requests, get advice, and seek assistance.
>
> **Coast Guard Mutual Assistance**—Major support and relief organization for Coast Guard service members, veterans, and families.

Enduring Freedom K.I.A. Fund—Gives financial aid to families of service members killed in action.

Fallen Patriot Fund—Accepts donations to send to families of those who fell in combat.

Global War on Terrorism Veterans In Need—Provides support programs for returning disabled service members.

Homes for Our Troops—Assists injured veterans and their families by building new or adapting existing homes for handicapped accessibility.

Navy/Marine Relief Society—Official support and relief organization for Navy service members, veterans, and families.

The Survivors of Servicemembers SOS Fund—Provides funds to families who have lost a loved one in Iraq

Veterans of Foreign Wars—Features a full range of veteran services and advocacy programs.

Wounded Warriors Fund—Donates everything from phone cards to TVs to wounded soldiers

Post Deployment/Mobilization Respite Absence Program

The Army Post Deployment/Mobilization Respite Absence program was designed to credit Soldiers who deploy to areas where they get Hostile Fire/Imminent Danger pay, with administrative leave dates.

Reserve Soldiers will be extended up to two years on active duty after a deployment so that they can use up their PDMRA leave days. If the Reserve Soldier is a federal, state or local government employee, and they do not want to be extended to use the leave days, they have the option of being paid a lump sum of up to $200 a day, but no more than $3000 a month for those days.

The PDMRA days have no cash value and should be requested using a DA Form 31, Request and Authority for Leave. Soldiers are advised to keep documentation, including mobilization or deployment orders, and/or their DD Form 214, as proof of entitlement from previous deployments or mobilizations.[25]

Conclusion: A Snowflake in the Desert

Tom sitting in the pilot seat of a Black Hawk combat helicopter.

I have often been asked to explain what is the most difficult part about being stationed in a combat and war zone. Is it the possibility of being killed? No. Is it the threats from enemies near and far? No. Is it the horrid drivers? No. Then it must be the numerous times I have traveled throughout the Iraq War Theater of operations? No.

The most difficult and challenging thing for me to deal with was being away from my family and in particular my children. When I was deployed in July 2006 to go to Iraq, (though I ended up in Kuwait), my son was 9 months old and my daughter was 4 years old. Upon my return home later this year, my son will be nearly 3 years old and my daughter will be 6 years old.

I missed a great deal of their early life as a result of my deployment. During the time I was deployed my son learned to walk, got his first hair cut, (though I took him to get his

1st "professional" hair cut when I returned home during one of my two R&R vacations.) My daughter lost her first tooth. However, the greatest disappointment was the fact I missed my daughter's entire year of Kindergarten.

Kindergarten is the time in a child's life when they learn a great deal about life. There have even been books written about the importance of Kindergarten on a person's life. One such book is entitled "*All I Ever Really Needed to Know I Learned in Kindergarten*"

Without sounding biased and proud, I have the smartest children in the world. Marissa without a doubt is a very bright little girl. I have often said she is 5 going on 26. She was reading at the age of 4. Most of all she is the epitome of a "Daddy's Girl". If you do not believe me, stop what you are doing, go to Webster's Dictionary and look up the definition of "Daddy's Girl". There amongst the words you will see a photo of Marissa looking back at you smiling.

While I was deployed, my daughter Marissa graduated from Kindergarten. Because of my deployment, I was unable to attend. However, I learned something very profound about my daughter. During the graduation ceremony or should I say "Celebration" the children received a DVD of their experiences in kindergarten as well as a yearbook.

Inside of the yearbook the teacher asked each of the students a question. The teacher asked the students to finish the following sentence; If I were a snowflake I would...

Of course all the students answered the question with all sorts of amusing responses. When I was informed how Marissa answered, it brought a tear to my eye and a tremendous sense of pride to my soul. My 5 year old daughter stated in response the following;

"If I were a Snowflake I would travel to the Army so I could be with my Dad!"

Well needless to say she will always be my little Snowflake in the desert. Even if the temperatures can and often do reach temperatures of 140 degrees or more in the summertime.

As you begin your deployment never forget the little things in life. It is those things that make the biggest memories.

Tom with Iraqi interpreter.

Final Thoughts

Across the United States, military service members are honored for the sacrifice and hard work they display everyday to protect this country's freedoms.

It is a great personal sacrifice to leave your loved ones, travel great distances, engage in combat and maintain the proud legacy of honor and dedication that has built our Armed Forces.

My two years of service in the Iraq combat theater of operations was the most difficult but most rewarding experience of my military career, and I will always be proud to have served.

For those of you who are about to serve, be proud. Be also encouraged by the fact that you can make it through this challenge, and hopefully you will be a better person for it. I hope the information presented in this book has helped you to be better prepared for what lies ahead. If Tom Mengesha can make it, so can you. You can reach me via e-mail at:

attorney.mengesha@gmail.com

Hooah!

Sources

Poision lead singer Bret Michaels with Tom.

1. www.military.com/benefits/resources/family-support/family-care
2. www.tricare.osd.mil
3. www.naccrra.org/MilitaryPrograms
4. www.militaryonesource.com/skins/MOS/home.aspx
5. www.ourmilitarykids.org/index.html
6. www.ourmilitarykids.org/programs/eligible_activities.html
7. www.ehow.com/how_2119433_pack-care-package-deployed-soldiers.html
8. usmilitary.about.com/cs/sscra/a/scra1.htm
9. usmilitary.about.com/od/glossarytermsm/g/m4112.htm
10. www.dix.army.mil/Directorate_Plans_Training_Mobilization/mobilization/opsinfochecklists/firstusarmy CGMemo.pdf
11. www.armyreserve.army.mil/ARWEB/ORGANIZATION/FACILITIES/Installations.htm
12. www.mccoy.army.mil/AboutFortMcCoy/History/index.asp?id=History
13. www.west-point.org/class/usma1995/classnews/IRR/What_to_do.doc
14. http://en.wikipedia.org/wiki/Kuwait
15. www.globalsecurity.org/military/facility/camp-buehring.htm

16. https://www.infantry.army.mil/welcomehome/content/guide/11_finance.pdf
17. http://en.wikipedia.org/wiki/Thrift_Savings_Plan
18. http://usmilitary.about.com/cs/moneymatters/a/savings.htm
19. www.armyg1.army.mil/randr/docs/About%20the%20Program.pdf
20. www.army.com/news/item/3595
21. www.qatartourism.gov.qa/leisure.html
22. http://usmilitary.about.com/od/theorderlyroom/a/citizenship.htm
23. www.military.com/benefits/resources/support-our-troops#1
24. http://en.wikipedia.org/wiki/Foxhole
25. www.dvidshub.net/?script=news/news_show.php&id=15996

Metal Sanaz and Tom

www.ingramcontent.com/pod-product-compliance
Lightning Source LLC
Chambersburg PA
CBHW071506040426
42444CB00008B/1518